Johnson J. Hooper

Twayne's United States Authors Series

Lewis Leary, Editor

University of North Carolina, Chapel Hill

TUSAS 454

JOHNSON J. HOOPER (1815–1862)
Photograph courtesy of the
Alabama Department of Archives and History

Johnson J. Hooper

By Paul Somers, Jr.

Michigan State University

Twayne Publishers • Boston

Johnson J. Hooper

Paul Somers, Jr.

Copyright © 1984 by G. K. Hall & Company
All Rights Reserved
Published by Twayne Publishers
A Division of G. K. Hall & Company
70 Lincoln Street
Boston, Massachusetts 02111

Book Production by Elizabeth Todesco
Book Design by Barbara Anderson

Printed on permanent/durable acid-free
paper and bound in the United States of
America.

**Library of Congress Cataloging in
Publication Data**

Somers, Paul.
    Johnson J. Hooper.

    (Twayne's United States authors series; TUSAS 454)
    Bibliography: p. 158
    Includes index.
    1. Hooper, Johnson Jones, 1815–1862.
    2. Authors, American—19th century—Biography.
    3. Journalists—United States—Biography.
    4. American wit and humor—History and criticism.
    5. Alabama in literature.
    I. Title.   II. Series.
PS1999.H25Z87 1984   813'.3   84–10874
ISBN 0–8057–7394–0

For my wife, Maribeth,
my children, Sarah and Keith,
and for my father and mother

Contents

About the Author

Paul Somers, Jr., is Professor of American Thought and Language at Michigan State University. He holds the Bachelor's and the Master's Degree in English from Miami University (Ohio) and the Ph.D. in English from the Pennsylvania State University.

He has published articles in the *South Atlantic Quarterly, Twentieth Century Literature,* and the *French Review,* among others, as well as a short story in *Harper's* and others in literary magazines. He is coauthor with Nancy Pogel of a bibliographical essay on "Editorial Cartooning" in volume 2 of *The Handbook of American Popular Culture.*

Preface

Over 120 years after the death of Johnson J. Hooper, his name is hardly a household word: "Johnson J. *Who?*" is the response of northerner and southerner, engineer and English professor alike. The originator of Simon Suggs, whose stories in the *Spirit of the Times* once made the nation laugh, whose *Adventures of Simon Suggs* went through eleven editions between 1845 and 1856, deserves a better fate.

Today he is sometimes studied as one of the best of the southwestern humorists, gentlemen professionals who in their spare time wrote humorous sketches about life in their region for local newspapers and the *Spirit.* They flourished in the frontier areas of the South Atlantic, Gulf, and Upper Southern states roughly from 1835 to the Civil War. Few, however, are remembered today, and of those, Johnson J. Hooper is not the best known. Among students of American literature, George Washington Harris, creator of the roguish Sut Lovingood, probably ranks first. The anonymous Davy Crockett and Mike Fink tales are doubtless familiar to a wider audience than the yarns either of Harris or Hooper. The southwestern humorists' popularity gradually faded after the Civil War, with only Samuel Clemens surviving to carry their vernacular style and comic realism into the new age of national humor.

For his part, Hooper was in his day nationally and even internationally hailed as the author of *Simon Suggs.* It was Hooper himself who turned away from his humor, before the public did. Within ten years of the "Shifty Man"'s appearance, his maker correctly surmised that a reputation as a humorist might hold him back as he sought to shape the destiny of his state and the South in general through partisan politics and as a pro–Southern Rights, anti–"Free-soil Northern Democratic" editor.

He did earn widespread regional respect as an editor in an illustrious career that climaxed with the founding and editing of the *Montgomery Mail.* Highly regarded as the "beau ideal of a first rate editor" in 1854, by 1860 he would be labeled "one of the most popular editors in the South" by the *Spirit.*

Concerning his strong support of secession, another paper averred that "the world does not contain a better nor a braver heart than throbs in the bosom of J. J. Hooper."

His public service alone would have been enough to make most people proud, as he was elected solicitor of the Ninth Judicial Circuit and secretary of the Provisional Confederate Congress. But partisan politics caught up with the man who, first as a Whig and then as a "Know-Nothing," had fought the "bogus Democrats" tooth and nail most of his adult life, and he died soon after being shunted aside. It would seem that his detractors among the Democrats had had the last word.

Ultimately, it is neither to his skillful editorship of the *Montgomery Mail* nor to his devoted service of the Confederate nation, which treated him rather shabbily in the end, that Hooper owes his limited but lasting fame. Ironically, the man who aspired to nobler things in public life is remembered for the whimsical product of his lighter moments, for the antihero of sketches tossed off originally to fill space in his newspapers.

The rascally Suggs, whose motto was "It is good to be shifty in a new country," is still appealing today. Armed only with mother wit, a jug of whiskey, and an uncanny knack for exploiting the "soft spots" in his fellow man's nature, he glides through the swamps and backwoods towns of frontier Alabama, one bloodshot eye peeled for the "main chance." Believing firmly in Providence, but helping it along whenever necessary, the Captain has ridden into American literary history—mounted on a fine horse obtained in a swap with a greenhorn.

Hooper's writing is intrinsically worthwhile. Aside from their humor and literary skill, his stories and sketches vividly portray the twilight of America's frontier period, when a man could beat up his neighbor and be assured of a trial by a jury of his peers—men who had at one time or other assaulted *their* neighbors. There was no government agency to protect the buyer of a lame horse or a wooden nutmeg. With Simon Suggses around, *everyone* had to beware.

In his editorials we read of a South increasingly frustrated by the industrial North with its rising tide of Catholic immigration. In his fiery words we trace the gradual elimination of all compromise until secession loomed as the only alternative. Through his increasingly indignant editorials about "abolitionist rascality'' and other outrages, we feel the national passions rising to a fever pitch. The slavery question aside, he shows us America teetering on the balance point between the homogeneous agrarian society of Thomas Jefferson, governed by a natural aristocracy, and the heterogeneous urban plutocracy of Martin Van Buren, ruled by the manipulated votes of the mob.

This study presents Hooper's work against the sketchy background of what is known about his life, diligently researched years ago by Marion Kelley and W. Stanley Hoole. I have quoted extensively from his writings, especially from the irregularly preserved and erratically microfilmed *Montgomery Mail.* (Other papers, such as the *Wetumpka Whig,* have fared still worse.) Aside from the 1969 Southern Literary Classics Series edition of *Adventures of Simon Suggs,* most of Hooper's stores are available only in the *Spirit of the Times* and the rare *The Widow Rugby's Husband.*

Through his writings and contemporary accounts is revealed a remarkable and complex man, one of intelligence, wit, compassion, and deep moral—abolitionism was considered a moral aberration in ''the land o' cotton''—and political conviction. It is due to the vagaries of literary and political fortune, not to any lack of talent or character, that he has failed to attain the renown he sought as a young man of twenty when he headed west to the frontier village of Lafayette, Alabama.

For their assistance in the preparation of this book, I would like to thank my editor, Lewis Leary; the staff of the Michigan State University Library, especially Anne Pitts and the Document Delivery Department, whom I bedeviled with my insistent requests for obscure newspapers; my typist, Judy Easterbrook; and Michigan State University for the All-University Research Grant that, along with typing funds from the Department of American Thought and Language, helped finance this work. Most of all, I would like to thank my family for putting up with my years of ''Hoopering.''

Paul Somers, Jr.

Michigan State University

Chronology

1855   Throws *Montgomery Mail*'s support to American or
        Know-Nothing party. *Read and Circulate: Proceedings of
        the Democratic and Anti–Know-Nothing Party, in Caucus.*

1856   Introduced to the Southern Commercial Convention as
        "Simon Suggs." *Dog and Gun: A Few Loose Chapters on
        Shooting.*

1859   Edits *Woodward's Reminiscences of the Creek, or Muscogee
        Indians.* Participates in unsuccessful effort to organize
        Alleghany Mining Company. Outspoken supporter of
        "Southern Rights."

1860   Advocates secession.

1861   Elected secretary of the Provisional Confederate Con-
        gress. Stops writing for the *Mail,* later sells his interest
        in it. Moves to Richmond when the government relo-
        cated. Joins the Catholic Church.

1862   Loses bid for election to secretaryship of the Senate of
        reorganized Confederate Congress. Given job of copy-
        ing the proceedings of the Provisional Congress. Dies
        of "lung disease" on June 7, in Richmond, Virginia.

Chapter One
The Early Years

A Fine Southern Family

The history of the Hoopers is a typical, if unusually distinguished, American story. Beginning with William Hooper, who brought the family name and an Edinburgh University master's degree from Scotland to Boston in 1737, the Hoopers boasted statesmen, authors, ministers, educators, and editors among their number. After nine years as pastor of Boston's West Congregational Church, William I journeyed to England, where he was ordained as a minister of the more liberal Episcopal faith. Back in Boston, he became rector of Trinity Church. Twenty years in this position gained him renown as a minister and theologian.[1]

Shortly before William's death in 1767, three of his sons, William, George, and Thomas, had moved south to Wilmington, North Carolina. Thomas fathered no children, but from William II and George, the grandfather of Johnson J. Hooper, descended two long lines of Hoopers.

Most notable of the three southern Hoopers was William II. Memorialized by his family and in history books as "the signer" and "the prophet of American Independence," he graduated Harvard A.B. in 1760 and A.M. in 1763. He later studied law with James Otis.[2] He soon returned to Wilmington, where he was prominent in North Carolina's struggle for independence, representing the state in the Continental Congress and signing the Declaration of Independence "in bold letters."[3]

In contrast, William's brother, George, Johnson's grandfather, was strongly loyalist. It is a tribute to the respect in which George Hooper was held by his neighbors that he was able to remain aloof from the movement for independence and yet retain his reputation and property intact. Indeed, he married Catherine Maclaine, the only daughter of Archibald Maclaine, an ardent

supporter of independence, who subsequently served in the
North Carolina state legislature. It was after this patriot that
George and Catherine Hooper named the eldest of their three
children, Archibald Maclaine Hooper.

Archibald, eventually to become the father of Johnson, began
his career promisingly enough, practicing law and serving as
solicitor of the Wilmington Circuit. In 1806 he married Charlotte DeBerniere, a great-granddaughter of the French Hu-
guenot hero Jean Antione DeBerniere and a direct descendant
of Jeremy Taylor, famous seventeenth-century English clergy-
man and religious writer. By 1815 she had borne six children,
the youngest of whom was Johnson Jones Hooper, born on
June 9, 1815. The family prospered because Archibald had in-
herited his father's plantation and salt works. He then left the
practice of law to become cashier of the Wilmington branch
of the North Carolina State Bank. In 1826 he changed professions again, purchasing the *Cape-Fear Recorder,* Wilmington's
only newspaper.

His ineptness at all practical pursuits had caught up with him
by 1832, as he was forced to sell the paper, even though he
had enjoyed editing and writing for it. His patrimony exhausted,
he took a position in the Wilmington Customs House. Upon
losing that job soon after, he had no choice but to move in
with his daughter, Louisa, in Pittsboro, North Carolina.

The older Hooper brothers enjoyed the benefits of the family's early prosperity: George attended West Point and ultimately
practiced law, and John graduated from the University of North
Carolina, where he later achieved eminence as a scholar of Greek
and Latin. Johnson, however, was left with the hardships of
their poverty. His formal education did not progress beyond
the Wilmington public school, but he had his father for a tutor.
Archibald was more at home with scholarship, for which he
had acquired a reputation, one not helpful to a lawyer in those
days, than with the various professions at which he had failed.
To these influences must be added the cultural one of Mrs.
Hooper. Also not to be overlooked is that classic training ground
for the American writer, the print shop: between the ages of
eleven and seventeen Johnson worked as a printer's devil for
the *Cape-Fear Recorder.*

It was precisely this connection with his father's newspaper

that gave fifteen-year-old Johnson J. Hooper the opportunity
to see his work in print. In early spring of 1830, the inhabitants
of the Cape Fear Peninsula turned out one afternoon to watch
the launching of the schooner *Hatteras.* Conspicuous by his bulk,
arrogance, and bemedaled splendor was Anthony Milan, the
highly unpopular British consul. At the moment of launching,
"Sir" Anthony waddled to the edge of the christening platform,
and other spectators joined him. Then occurred the event that
gave young Johnson the occasion for his first published comic
observation of a fellow human:

> Just at that moment when she stopped,
>   With many a shake and shiver,
> The pompous British consul slipped
>   And tumbled in the river.
>
> The Cape Fear rose three feet or more
>   As Anthony went under
> The waves they beat upon the shore
>   In peals of living thunder.[4]

When it appeared in the *Recorder,* the twenty-one-stanza poem,
"Anthony Milan's Launch," was well received by the residents
of Wilmington and the Cape Fear region.

In that same year Johnson's older brother, George, left Wilmington to practice law in Charleston. By 1835, he was settled
in Lafayette, "chief city" of Chambers County, East Alabama.
For reasons that are not altogether clear, Johnson then left home,
perhaps after a family dispute. More likely, it was a combination
of the reversal of his father's fortunes and his admiration of
the brother who had helped tutor him in the law that led young
"Jonce" to leave the comparative refinement of Wilmington
for the frontier village of Lafayette, whose buildings were log
cabins and whose streets were mud.

Flush Times

Joseph G. Baldwin entitled his popular collection of humorous
stories *Flush Times in Alabama and Mississippi* (New York, 1853),
and flush those times were. Even though Lafayette had a population of barely two hundred when Hooper arrived in 1835, and

the entire county of Chambers only twelve thousand or so, the piney woods and the red clay seemed to promise a livelihood, and more, to all. By 1840, the census showed that 17,333 persons had settled in Chambers County.

Among the flood of settlers pouring in from eastern Alabama, Virginia, Tennessee, Georgia, and the Carolinas were migrants of every description. Most numerous were those traditionally thought of as pioneers, hard-working families who migrated west in search of elbow room and fertile soil. It was these people—farmers, printers, mechanics, carpenters, blacksmiths, and merchants—who would break the back of the wilderness, clear the farms, and populate the towns of the new territory.

Others, much fewer in number, also came seeking success. These, however, were leaving behind prosperity in the form of plantations, law or medical practices, newspapers, or teaching jobs. Like George Hooper and his brother Johnson, they sensed in the new country's lure the promise of adventure and even greater accomplishment.

A third group, one that likely outnumbered the second, was the fugitives. Some were literally fugitives from justice: according to W. Stanley Hoole, Hooper's biographer, "It might have been frontier etiquette to ask a settler whence or even how he came to Alabama—but never *why.*" Others were ex-convicts, and still others were simply fleeing a society that was becoming too stratified and restrictive for them.

Somewhere in this group must be ranked the poor whites, sometimes called "dirt-eaters." They were not especially dishonest—perhaps that required too much effort—just poorly educated and poorly nourished. They seemed to prove that some people would manage to fail anywhere. Their very name was an insult, and Hooper would years hence write a sketch called "The Dirtiken," in which a scrawny poor white youth tries to match wits with a burly ring-tailed roarer type. The lad is described as a twin brother to Judge Longstreet's archetypal cracker, Ransy Sniffle. When he announces that he is an American soldier, the man professes to disbelieve him, saying he must be a "Dirtiken" because he eats so much dirt. The bystanders laugh and the boy slinks away. Later, he is boasting over some whiskey in a "grocery" store, when the man returns. He is afraid at first, but the man is conciliatory and apologizes. With five hundred men like you, he says, he could take "the city of Mexico." Flattered, the boy listens enraptured while the ringtail unfolds his plan. What he would do is have his special force surround the city, without guns, and then give the order. "What order?" the gullible boy asks.

"Why, the order, Dig and Eat!" The special regiment of dirt-eaters could eat its way through the walls "like so many gophers." Again, the poor white boy is laughed out of the place.[5]

A final component of the frontier population was the Creek Indians. The Creeks had come to western Alabama long before the whites, but this did them little good. As long as they held title to land, they were relentlessly pursued by speculators, who used every means to induce the Indians to sign over their land: they plied them with whiskey; greedy, unscrupulous men married the Creeks' daughters, gained control of their property, then deserted them.

As they lost their grip on their land and their traditional way of life, the Creeks were not exactly welcomed by the white settlers. The majority, who were attempting to prosper without taking advantage of the naive native Americans, regarded them as something between a threat and a nuisance. Contemporary accounts tell of their drinking and begging, and court records show Indians being tried for crimes as serious as murder.

Johnson J. Hooper sympathized so strongly with their plight that he later became known as the "Champion of the Creeks." Nostalgically recalling the great Indian Council of 1835, when five thousand Indians lit the night with their campfires, Hooper denounced the speculators who had cheated them so shamelessly that, when the Creeks were transported from the area, many were paupers and had to be carried off in government wagons for the poor. In the Suggs tale "Simon Speculates Again," Hooper would note with great satisfaction the fate of these swindlers:

And where are these speculators now?—those lords of the soil—men of dollars—the fortune-makers who bought with hundreds what was worth thousands!—they to whom every revolution of the sun brought a reduplication of their wealth! Where are they, and what are they, now! They have been smitten by the hand of retributive justice! The curse of their victims has fastened upon them, and nine out of ten are houseless, outcast, bankrupt! In the flittings of ten years, the larger portion have lost money, lands, character, every thing! And the few who still retain something of their once lordly possessions, mark its steady, unaccountable diminution, and strive vainly to avert their irresistible fate—an old age of shame and beggary. They are cursed, all of them—blighted, root and trunk and limb! The Creek is avenged![6]

The crossroads society of such places as Chambers County proved the perfect melting pot for this wide variety of Americans. For the well-educated lawyer, doctor, editor, surveyor, and so forth, to prosper, he had to avoid giving the slightest impression he thought himself better than the "crackers," "dirt-eaters," "red-necks," "hill-billies," or "peckerwoods" with whom he found it necessary to associate. Hospitality was the law of the land: to fail to leave one's latchstring out for the chance visitor or, worse, to lock a door was considered terrible manners. Carrying concealed weapons, fighting with a gun or knife, and picking on a smaller man were frowned upon, but fist-fighting was practically the order of the day among the hard-working, hard-drinking men of the frontier.

By way of diversion, the rude frontier community offered little beyond "tippling houses" and grocery stores that sold whiskey by the dipperful. From time to time, however, such occasions as weddings, camp meetings, cock fights, quilting bees, funerals, and such helped relieve the monotony of day-to-day existence.

It was in this raucous, free-wheeling society of Lafayette, Alabama, then, that twenty-year-old Johnson J. Hooper had to make his way. His primary responsibility was to read the law in his brother's office in order to prepare himself for eventual partnership with George, who had in his two years in Chambers County established himself firmly as an attorney, a businessman, and a slave-owner.

As the brother of George Hooper, Johnson had social access to the members of Lafayette's upper crust, and George's friends took an immediate liking to "jolly, fun-loving Johnson." One of these men, Bird H. Young, was later accorded the dubious honor of serving in part as a model for Johnson's famous rascal, Simon Suggs.

The upper crust of this frontier outpost was quite thin, however, and young Johnson had ample opportunity to sample the filling and the lower crust. Yeoman farmers, along with such tradesmen as storekeepers, blacksmiths, mechanics, carpenters, and the like, made up the bulk of the population. Also well represented were those whose vocations were less apparent, who lived upon the land without cultivating it, or who frequented the town without conducting any commerce other than gambling, buying liquor, or perhaps swapping horses. From these, Hooper doubtless borrowed traits with which to flesh out Simon's character and antics to furnish his adventures.

The Chicken Man

In September 1837, Hooper accompanied a friend, Joseph A. Johnson, to Texas on some family business. By fall of 1838, he had returned and was sworn in as a notary public in adjoining Tallapoosa County. He apparently practiced law there and in Dadeville until 1840, when he was deputized as an assistant marshall and given the job of taking the census of Tallapoosa County.

He was to count not only the county's human inhabitants, but also its chickens. Thus, it was as "the chicken man" that young Hooper ranged the nine hundred square miles of rugged terrain. The residents received him suspiciously at best, and some set their dogs on him, fearing that taxation would follow close on his heels. If there was anything about his fellow Alabamians that he had failed to learn in the taverns or at the quarter-horse races, he certainly found it out during his month-long course of recording the county's 2,318 white males, 2,106 white females, 2,013 slaves, and nine free colored persons. The task proved to be harder than he had anticipated, for he subsequently filed a request for higher compensation. (The government's response has been lost.) Three years later, however, he turned the experience into the tale that would launch his career as a nationally known humorist.

Shortly after, Hooper entered into the practice of law with a friend, Charles Stone. Surviving records show that they had some clients, but they nevertheless dissolved the partnership. In mid-1842, Johnson joined his brother's law firm in Lafayette. "G. & J. Hooper, Attorneys at Law" practiced in Chambers

and Tallapoosa counties, but Johnson devoted much of his attention to Lafayette.

It was romance, as much as the law, that interested him there,
for he was courting Ann E. Brantley, the older daughter of
wealthy planter Green D. Brantley. When she married Thomas
R. Heard instead, Hooper reportedly was broken-hearted. He
began to pay attention to her younger sister, Mary, and they
were married on December 15, 1842, just one month after
the wedding of Thomas and Ann.

A mere two days later occurred yet another event that would
greatly affect Hooper's life: the Lafayette printing firm of John
F. Gilbert & Son put out what was apparently the initial issue
of the *East Alabamian,* the first newspaper in Chambers County.
The best available evidence suggests that Hooper became the
paper's first editor. He then left his brother George's firm and
announced in the *East Alabamian* that he intended to practice
law and could be found at the newspaper's office.

Thus, at age twenty-six, Hooper found many strands of his
life and heritage coming together. He had been groomed by
his father and brother for the practice of law. Like his great-
uncle William, "the prophet of American independence," he
craved political involvement; in the years to come, his editorial
position would be staunchly Whig. Still later, as the tensions
leading to the Civil War increased, he would advocate states'
rights up to and including secession. Once a printer's devil on
his father's paper, he was now editor of his own paper. The
wit that had won him so many friends and had manifested itself
early in the precocious poem "Anthony Milan's Launch" would
soon find an outlet in the newspaper tales of Simon Suggs, which
would win him national attention. As a matter of fact, there
would come a time, some fourteen years hence, when his fame
as the creator of Simon Suggs would prove downright embarrass-
ing to him, and he would regard the popularity of the backwoods
trickster as a definite hindrance to his career in public life.

Chapter Two

"It Is Good to Be Shifty in a New Country"

Young Hooper threw himself enthusiastically into his new job as editor of the weekly *East Alabamian.* He immediately announced the paper's loyalty to the Whig party.

The origins of the Whigs, a major political party since the mid-1830s, lay in the old National Republican party, which had supported John Quincy Adams and Henry Clay. They stood for federal promotion of national economic development and vigorously opposed Andrew Jackson and the strident egalitarianism of many of his followers. They tended to be more cosmopolitan than the Jacksonians and included among their number practitioners of large-scale agriculture and manufacturing and those who felt they would profit from increased internal commerce encouraged by the federally chartered Second Bank of the United States. The Whig party was at best an uneasy coalition, its ranks swelled as they were from time to time by defecting Jacksonians, such as the states' rights Calhounites from South Carolina, and by special interest groups like the Anti-Masons.

When Johnson J. Hooper ran up the Whig banner on the front page of the *East Alabamian* in 1842, that party was at the peak of its power, William Henry "Tippecanoe" Harrison having defeated the Democrat, Martin Van Buren, in the presidential election of 1840. Alabama, however, had gone Democratic. Hooper's old friend Joseph A. Johnson, with whom he had traveled to Texas a few years earlier, was one Democrat who canceled his subscription to the *East Alabamian.*

In addition to his own pro-Whig editorials, Hooper also reprinted material culled from other newspapers in the fashion of the day. More important, however, he printed some of his own work and soon gained a reputation for wit. One of these pieces spread his name and fame farther than the young country editor had even dared dream.

Back in 1840, when he had crisscrossed Tallapoosa County as an assistant marshall, Hooper had had many adventures, which he now recalled in a humorous manner. On August 5 or 28 he published in his paper "Taking the Census in Alabama," which he signed "By a Chicken Man of 1840."

Adventures of a Chicken Man

"Part First" of "Taking the Census" begins with the educated narrator's explanation of his task, "to count the noses of all the men, women, children, and chickens resident upon those nine hundred square miles of rough country which constitute the county of Tallapoosa."[1] The self-deprecating narrator is never named, although some of the citizens he counts call him " 'squire." We know he is Johnson J. Hooper, though, from biographical evidence and from the similarities between his physical appearance and contemporary accounts of Hooper: one old woman calls him a "long-legged, hatchet-faced whelp" (153), and a mother declares him "the *slimmest* critter, to be sure ever I seed" (169).

The squire had expected his task to be "glorious sport." However, the experiences were, "at the time, anything but mirth-inspiring to us" (150), as he came close to being drubbed a dozen times, "and only escaped by a very peculiar knack we have of 'sliding out' " (150).

The first adventure he recounts is his attempt to tabulate the family and possessions of "a widow rather past the prime of life—just that period at which nature supplies most abundantly the oil which lubricates the hinges of the female tongue" (150–51). She gruffly assures him that her dogs, "wolfish curs" to our census taker, just a week ago killed a two-year-old steer. Her hostility toward the chicken man is exceeded only by her outright hatred of Democratic President Martin Van Buren:

"Kill him! kill him—oh—if I had him here by the *years* I reckon I *would* kill him. A pretty fellow to be eating his vittils out'n gold spoons that poor people's taxed for, and raisin' an army to get him made king of Ameriky—the oudacious, nasty, stinking old scamp!" (152–53)

Not surprisingly, since "Taking the Census" first appeared in Hooper's Whig newspaper, the old woman's attack on Van Buren for prodigality with the people's wealth echoes the Whigs' successful propaganda from the election of 1840.

The irascible woman refuses to tell him more than the number of her children and insists that he enter her in his ledger simply as "Judy Tompkins, *ageable* woman, and four children" (153). He refuses at first, giving in when she threatens to set her dogs on him. Safely remounted on his horse, he makes a rude gesture and shouts that she would make a good match in marriage for a lame gentleman of his acquaintance. She finally does set the dogs on him, but he canters off, the hounds snapping futilely at his horse's heels.

Next the "little 'squire" encounters Sol Todd, a rustic trickster who, pretending to direct the stranger to a safe ford, sends him into a deep hole, where his horse must swim and drench him. Learning shortly after that Sol had boasted he would make the chicken man take a swim, the squire returns and turns the tables on the joker. He tells Sol that he lost a buckskin pouch containing twenty-five dollars in gold in the swirling current. If Sol will retrieve it from the September-chilled stream, they will share the money equally. "Sol soon denuded himself and went under the water in the 'Buck Hole' like a shuffler duck with his wing broke." The squire excuses himself, saying he is in a hurry, and bids Sol to bring the pouch and half the money to Dadeville when he finds it. We last see blue, shivering Sol diving for the nonexistent money pouch. The narrator notes with placid cruelty that "the 'river ager' made Sol shake worse than that, that fall" (157).

Moving on, he gives a pretty young lady, "a buxom one of twenty" (157), some dubious advice concerning President Van Buren's plans to buy chickens and feed the roosters to the officers to make them brave. "She was perfectly delighted, and we do not hesitate to say, would have rewarded us with a kiss, if we had asked it; but in those days modesty was the bright trait in our character" (158).

He next encounters an old lady as agreeable as the first one was disagreeable. She gets the best of the chicken man by dint of her amiability and extreme loquaciousness. Her endless digressions wear out his patience as he continues to press her for the dollar value of her chickens, whose number she will estimate only as "nigh" about the same as last year. Finally, she throws out a handful of corn to lure her fowl and invites him to see for himself. He is engulfed by "a din and confusion altogether indescribable." But she refuses to say what they are worth; "no persuasion could bring her to the point; and our papers at Washington contain no estimate of the value of the widow Stokes' poultry, although, as she said herself, she had *'a mighty nice passel!'* " (164).

"Part Second" of "Taking the Census" introduces old Kit Kuncker, perhaps Hooper's best-developed character with the exception of Simon Suggs. "Old Kit was a fine specimen of the old-fashioned Georgia wagoner, of the glorious old times when locomotives didn't whiz about in every direction," Hooper writes nostalgically. "Uncle Kit was sixty years old, we suppose, but the merriest old dog alive; and his chirruping laugh sounded every minute in the day." He delights in plaguing the women of the settlement. "His waggery, of one sort or other, was incessant; and as he was the patriarch of his neighbour-hood—having transplanted every family in it, with himself, from Georgia—his jokes were all considered good jokes, and few dared be offended at his good-humored satire. Besides all this, Uncle Kit was a devoted Jackson man, and an inveterate hater of all nullifiers" (165). (In 1832 Congress passed a tariff bill that South Carolina, led by John C. Calhoun, opposed. Delegates to a special state convention declared the tariffs of 1828 and 1832 "unauthorized by the Constitution" and therefore "null, void, and no law, nor binding upon this State, its officers or citizens." President Jackson threatened to use military force, and South Carolina eventually agreed to a compromise on the tariff, but held fast to the principle of nullification.)

Uncle Kit invites the squire, whom he likes ("bless your little *union* snake skin"), to a wedding that next Thursday at the Kuncker house, the only frame building on Union Creek.

The squire arrives, bringing some census blanks, and is greeted by Uncle Kit. The old wagoner teases his wife by refer-ring to her as an "old dried-up witch," and a victim of the *"big ugly"* and urges her to cover her face with a meal bag or her apron, to spare the sensibilities of their guest. Mrs. Kuncker placidly urges the squire to come in, "or that poor light-headed old crittur 'ill laugh hisself to death!" (168).

His mind on his business, our narrator approaches a woman who is watching a small, half-naked child splash in a puddle apparently of his own making. The pattern of Hooper's Whig-tinged fun becomes evident here: since Kit Kuncker is a Jackson man, his dog's name is Andy. The baby's name is Thomas Jefferson (Naron), and his freedom from diapers is *sans culottism.* (*Sans-culotte*—"without breeches." The revolutionaries during the French Revolution wore pantaloons instead of the knee breeches worn by the upper classes.) The woman marvels at the squire's thinness and then spanks young Thomas Jefferson for splashing her. Impressed with the severity of the punishment, the squire relents in his questioning, "for we were convinced that the government did not expect its officers to run the risk of what Master Thomas Jefferson had got, merely to add another dozen yards of cloth, or score of chickens, to the estimated wealth of the country!" (170).

At this point, one of the young persons "commenced singing to a tune whiningly dolorous, nasal, unvaried, and interminable, the popular ditty of 'The Old Bachelare.' " We are treated to several verses, and Andy joins in until his howling deteriorates to a series of barks. Kit professes to be alarmed: "my poor dog has got *tangled up* in that *cussed* tune, and 'ill choke hisself to death!" (175). The vocalist leaves in a huff, "buttoning up his blue swallow-tail, and sleeking down his greasy locks." Aunt Hetty contributes her share to the confusion by pouring boiling water through a crack in the floor onto the musical dog Andy, who has taken refuge under the house.

Things calm down long enough for 'squire Berry to unite the nuptial couple "after the most summary fashion." Then Uncle Kit invites the guests to sit down for some "cold scraps," his modest way of referring to a frontier feast of "one or two half-grown hogs baked brown; two or three very fat turkeys; a hind quarter of beef; together with about a half-wagon-load of bread, cake, pies, stewed fruit, and so forth." Seeing a chance for mischief, Uncle Kit seats the chicken man next to Miss Winny Folsom, "a very pretty girl, with a pouting mouth": "here's a little gal has never had her *sensis* taken, and I want you to see ef you kan't git 'em, yah! yah!" (176–77).

Old Kit's chief aim is to stir up the jealousy of her swain, one Ikey Hetson,

a rare specimen of the piney-woods species of the genus homo. His face was not unhandsome, but he had a considerable stoop of the shoulders, and was knock-kneed to deformity. His coat was "blue-mixed," with a very acute terminus, and it seemed to have a particular affection for the hump of his shoulders, for it touched no other part of his person. (177)

Kit urges the squire to talk to the maid and, when their heads droop close together, he makes a great smacking noise with his lips and carries on as if the squire had kissed her. Teased by Uncle Kit, the youth works himself into a fury: "I kin whip any pocket-knife lawyer that ever made a moccasin track in *Datesville.*"

Miss Winny herself is none too sympathetic toward Ikey: "The 'squire's mouth aint *pisen,* I reckon . . . and it wouldn't *kill* a body if he *did* kiss 'em!" At this point our squire, apparently having recovered from the modesty he boasted of earlier, steals a kiss from Miss Winny.

Uncle Kit is transported with delight, Miss Winny is not displeased, and the jealous suitor seems about to turn ring-tail roarer: " 'Dern my everlastin dog-skin ef I'll stand it! . . . I'll die in my tracks fust! I'm jist as good as town folks, if they *do* war shoe-boots and store close. I'm jist a hunderd and forty *seving* pound, *neat* weight, and I'm a wheel-horse!' and then Mr. Hetson doubled his fists and shook himself all over, with an energy that looked dangerous . . ." (179).

The story verges upon violence, but in the next line Hooper's anticlimactic style neatly deflates the tension: "considered in reference to the excessive tightness of his buff cassimeres." The risk, then, is not of bodily harm to the squire, but rather of social embarrassment should the lad's tight pants split. Hetson makes a rush for the chicken man but is restrained by Kit Kuncker, who holds him by the shoulder while he delivers the coup de grace: *"You'll—tar—them—trousers!"*

This prediction defuses the situation, as Hetson is "used up," but old Kit has yet another way to make mischief. It seems that Andy, whose singing has proved so remarkable, can also tell the future. In a drawn-out passage, Andy divines that Miss Winny is going to marry the squire, rather than Ikey Hetson. Hetson receives the verdict very ungraciously and kicks the psychic canine in the ribs. Kit sets the dog on him, and chaos resumes:

Andy dashed gallantly at Mr. Hetson, and seizing one of his red-leather straps, tore it on one side from the buff cassimere, which,

frightened from "its propriety" by the display of canine teeth, re-
treated, instanter, to the neighbourhood of Mr. Hetson's knee! In
his struggle to get away from the dog, Ike fell backwards over Master
Thomas Jefferson Naron; and as his bare and unstrapped leg flew
up, nearly at right angles with his body—while its fellow, held quiet
by leather and cassimere, lay rigid along the floor—an uproarious
shout of laughter at the grotesque spectacle shook the whole house.
(187)

The result of this comic confusion is that Ikey leaves in disgrace
for "the Arkansaw" and, the narrator reflects uncompassion-
ately, "As for Winny—the little fool!—she wept bitterly, as if
there were no straight-legged men that would have been glad
to marry her!" (187).

The tale ends as Uncle Kit lights the squire to bed, promising
to show him around the settlement and tell him a few stories
in the bargain: "And 'squire, ef you want one o' Andy's puppies,
let yer uncle Kit know, and he'll save you a real *peart* one,
eh? Good night! God bless the old Ginnul, and damn all nullifiers!" (188).

"Taking the Census" is representative of the southwestern
humorous sketch. Like the other gentlemen humorists, Hooper
was widely read and was probably familiar with Boccaccio's
Decameron, Chaucer's *Canterbury Tales,* and the *Arabian Nights,*
all of which utilized a narrative frame for presenting an oral
tale. Hooper had not yet arrived at the use of this narrative
frame technique, however. A distinctive feature of "Taking the
Census" is the way in which the narrator himself continues in
the story and takes part in the adventures, sometimes besting,
sometimes being bested by the rather formidable folks he meets
in his travels.

Even though he does not remove himself from the story,
Hooper's narrator is nonetheless distinct from the common folk
with whom he must mix in order to witness their antics and
pass them on to his literate readers. Uncle Kit defers to him
as " 'squire," a shortening of *esquire,* the English term for a
lawyer or country gentleman.

Like most of the other writing lawyers, editors, doctors, and
planters of the time, Hooper admired and emulated the style
of Addison and Steele, famous English essayists and editors.

A column by Hooper in the *Montgomery Mail* for December 6, 1858, expresses delight at finding evidence in a deceased friend's bookshop that his "favorite," Addison, "was appreciated before the days of 'Noay Webster,' to-wit in the year 1721" (2, col. 1).

Not surprisingly, then, the very language of Hooper's erudite narrator sets him apart from the backwoods residents of Tallapoosa County. What a native would express as "sicced the dogs on" becomes "appealed to the couchant whelps." At another point, when a woman says she "didn't weave no cloth," the chicken man corrects her grammar. His farewell salute to the nasty woman consists of "placing our thumb on the nasal extremity of our countenance" (153). In the contrast between this bit of circumlocution and old Kit Kuncker's description of a woman "so ugly the flies won't light on her face" (188) lies the tension that gives southwestern humor its vitality.[2]

Hooper reproduces phonetically much of the colloquial dialogue of his subjects, enclosing it in quotation marks and occasionally italicizing especially "choice" bits of vernacular: "The children will suffer, I'm mightily *afeerd*" (159). He generally sticks to the contrasting styles and thus maintains the narrator's distance from the other characters. At one point, however, while making up to buxom Miss Betsy, the narrator himself slips into the vernacular: "Well, now, Miss Betsy," said we, "you know how much I set by the old man your daddy—and the old lady, you know how *she and me* [italics Hooper's]—and Jim and Dave, you know we was always like brothers—. . ." (157).

Anticipating Mark Twain, this confusion of levels of diction, even though the narrator is clearly condescending to the rustic lass, is symptomatic of the problems that arise when the narrator participates in the action. What appealed to readers was the raw lure of the frontier. A civilized narrator provided a frame or stabilizing point of reference for the story and assured the readers that all was under control, that anarchy would not spill over.

But what happens when the narrator is in the story, when he allows himself to speak ungrammatically to one young woman, and when he actually kisses another? And what of the menacing Ikey Hetson? For all his comic bumptiousness and precariously tight pants, he is physically formidable; the narrator and therefore the civilized reader sit across a narrow table from the belligerent Ikey. Without Uncle Kit to intervene, we must fear for the safety of our little squire.

Hooper would resolve this problem of narrative distance later, partly through the use of the narrative frame. When he conceived of a character tough and resourceful enough to have exciting adventures yet escape even the tightest scrape, and preserved his educated narrator to insulate the reader from anarchy and disorder, when he conceived of Simon Suggs, he would move into the very front ranks of the southwestern humorists.

Our Alabama Correspondent

Having published "Taking the Census in Alabama" to entertain and simply to fill space, always a pressing problem for an editor, Hooper was unprepared for the reception that awaited his tale. A copy of the *East Alabamian* reached New York City, where it was read by William T. Porter, who was always alert for "correspondents" for the *Spirit of the Times.* Porter had founded this periodical, subtitled a "chronicle of the Turf, Agriculture, Field Sports, Literature and the Stage," in 1831. By 1843, he boasted some 16,000 subscribers, a substantial number for that time, scattered "from Hudson's Bay to the Caribbean Sea, from the shores of the Atlantic to the Pacific."[3] The publication's primary focus was on sports, especially the gentlemanly ones, and over the years Porter printed an increasing number of stories on sporting topics. Many of these were set in the Southwest, where the tallest tales about hunting, fishing, horse racing, and so forth were being told. By association, the Southwest itself became a region of interest to readers around the country.

When he saw "Taking the Census," Porter was delighted and reprinted it in the *Spirit.* (Obtaining the author's permission or paying him was unheard of at the time. Besides, the "correspondents" of the *Spirit* were gentlemen first and writers second.) With complimentary comparisons to established humorists, Porter introduced the story and its hitherto unknown author to his readers and to the nation on September 9, 1843: "The fol-

lowing graphic description of the denizens of a remote district
of country is copied from the 'East Alabamian,' . . . edited
with signal ability by Johnson J. Hooper, Esq. . . . This Hooper
is a clever man, and we must enlist him among the correspondents of the 'Spirit of the Times' . . ." (12:326).

After the manner of the time, Hooper answered in the pages
of the *East Alabamian.* He thanked Porter for republishing the
sketch and for his compliments, modestly demurring: "We suspect that we know our own calibre pretty well—and we are
small in the bore." He promised to contribute again to the
Spirit, and thus began an editorial friendship that was to last
until Porter's death in 1858, although it waned in later years.
"Taking the Census" caught on nationally, and the *Washington
News* and *Planters Gazette* reprinted it on October 5, and the
Columbus [Ga.] *Enquirer* on October 18, although neither
seemed aware that the "Chicken Man" was Johnson J. Hooper.

Once he had discovered an author, Porter was eager to share
him with the *Spirit*'s readers. So, when "Our Hunt Last Week"
appeared in the *East Alabamian* for December 2, 1843, he snap-
ped it up, retitled it "A Three Day's Hunt in Alabama," appended a flattering introduction, and included it in the *Spirit*
for December 23 (13:505).

Tall Tales

The tall tale is considered by many to be the oldest American
art form. It seems the earliest European colonists had no more
landed in the New World than they were writing home lies,
or at least shameless exaggerations, of its bountifulness. John
Smith solemnly maintained, "He is a very bad fisher [who]
cannot kill in one day with his hook and line one, two, or
three hundred cods. . . ."[6] Benjamin Franklin wrote for the
Public Advertiser in 1765 a letter from "A Traveler," who boasted
of America's bounty: "The very Tails of the American Sheep
are so laden with Wool, that each has a Car or Waggon on
four little Wheels to support and keep it from trailing on the
ground." The Canadian portion of Britain's North American
colony shared in this abundance, for the traveler assures the
reader

that the Inhabitants of Canada are making Preparations for a Cod and Whale Fishery this Summer in the Upper Lakes. Ignorant People may object that the Upper Lakes are fresh, and that Cod and Whale are Salt-water Fish: But let them know, Sir, that Cod, like other Fish, when attacked by their Enemies, fly into any Water where they think they can be safest; that Whales, when they have a Mind to eat Cod, pursue them wherever they fly; and that the grand Leap of the Whale in that Chace up the Fall of Niagara is esteemed by all who have seen it, as one of the finest Spectacles in Nature![7]

In the early and mid-nineteenth century the southwestern frontier abounded with tall-tale tellers, some who became legendary for their imagination. Around Whig congressman Davy Crockett sprang up countless tales, some of them originating in campaign literature and oratory. Crockett is still remembered for his ability to grin a squirrel out of a tree. He allegedly picked his teeth with a pitchfork and fanned himself with a hurricane. Nearly as famous was Mike Fink, King of the Riverboatmen, famed as a brawler and marksman. No shrinking violet was his daughter, Sal Fink, the Mississippi Screamer, who supposedly rode down the river on an alligator's back, standing upright and dancing "Yankee Doodle."

Southwestern humorists writing during and after the flourishing of such tall tales naturally made much use of this oral art form they heard practiced all around them. Hooper's contemporary Thomas Bangs Thorpe, a Yankee painter, editor, and writer transplanted to Louisiana, achieved fame with his story "The Big Bear of Arkansas." After telling how he bagged the "unhuntable bear," Thorpe's hunter placidly assures the reader that it took six men to load the carcass onto a mule. And the skin made a bedspread so big it covered an ordinary bearskin mattress with several feet left over on each side to tuck up.[8]

Lawyers and judges, traveling the rural court circuits as they did, were prime collectors and tellers of amusing yarns. Walter Blair in his introduction to *Native American Humor* lists ten of the most prominent southwestern humorists and points out that four of them, Augustus Baldwin Longstreet, Sol Smith, Joseph G. Baldwin, and Johnson J. Hooper, were lawyers.[9] Hooper was to write several tall tales, the first of which follows:

"A Three Day's Hunt in Alabama" purports to tell the adventures of Hooper, his dog, Pont, and three friends. The year of the hunt might be 1843, but the spirit of the tale is modern in that these are not frontiersmen, not Boones or Crocketts, but rather city gentlemen who have had little excitement or exercise for nearly two years and are ready to cut loose, to drink and yell and have a good time.

In "A Three Day's Hunt" Hooper employs the editorial "we." As in "Taking the Census," the diction is formal. "Our dreams at the moment were of them [the whoops of joy], . . . of the crackling leaf and the glistening frost; so giving a responsive yell we burst out of bed, encased our spindles, and in fifteen minutes, were in the free brown forest, on our way to the swamps of the Oakchun-hatchee, with three of the best fellows that ever shot deer or broke the neck of a wine bottle." When Hooper is lowering the level of his diction, he lets the readers know: "We have been told *'That thar were bar' '*" (italics Hooper's).

The hunters have a run-in with a mother bear and a cub, which they rout. A second cub sticks its head out of the hole. Their rules of sportsmanship seem rather lax, as "Sam" splits the cub's skull with one blow of his axe. They are forced to camp that night in swampy country, the scene of an eyebrow-raising adventure. Hooper prepares his readers as follows: "During that dismal night, a circumstance occurred which may appear incredible, but which we solemnly aver to be as true as any other part of this story."

Having given fair warning, Hooper recounts the exploit of his faithful dog. Pont, he claims, has developed a "mortal antipathy" for ducks, because the tame ones at home steal food from his dish. Therefore, he awakens his master at midnight and leads him to a flock of ducks, "as they 'rode at anchor' near the shore, like a fleet of little boats." In action suggestive of an animated cartoon, Pont approaches each duck in turn, touches its tail with his forepaw, and, when the duck takes its head from under its wing, he crushes its head in his jaws, before it can sound the alarm. In this fashion, Pont dispatches twenty-seven "fine fat ducks" and piles them before his master.

The tale gets taller and the dog shaggier, and, after recounting their final adventure, the killing of a wild boar and five attendant hogs, Hooper tallies up their take for the hunt:

(Final Tally)

Carcass of Bear (nett)	80 lbs.
42 Ducks (say) 1 lb (nett)	42 "
3 Turkeys (say) 12 lbs each	36 "
Old Boar (nett)	283 "
5 other Hogs	568 "
The Doe	49 "

making the nett weight of game killed by four persons, in two days, of *One Thousand and Fifty-eight Pounds!*[10]

This claim is rather modest, however, in light of Davy Crockett's boast of shooting "six cord" of bear in one day.

Impatient that no more stories were forthcoming from his Alabama correspondent, Porter reprinted excerpts from "A Three Day's Hunt" four months later. The episode, retitled "The Biters Bit," concerned Pont's duck-hunting exhibition. Porter rapturously exclaimed: "Col. Hooper of the 'East Alabamian' has a dog name 'Ponto' [*sic*] whose sagacity and exploits deserve to be handed down to posterity in 'perpetual verse' as much as the exploits of Achilles or the intrigues of Paris."[11]

Eager for material by Hooper, Porter even picked up the *Alabamian's* advertisement for his law practice and reprinted it in the *Spirit* on January 18, 1845:

L-A-W—L-A-W

The undersigned not having been elected by the legislature now in session to any office whatsoever, notwithstanding there were several which he might be induced to accept; and being extremely desirous to earn a subsistence by some Lawful means; announces to the public, that from and after this date, he will hold himself in readiness to serve all of his fellow citizens who may choose to entrust to him their

LAW BUSINESS

to the extent of his ability. (14:558)

Beneath Hooper's customary tone of self-satire is a note of financial need that reflects altered circumstances in the life of young Johnson. As mentioned in chapter 1, he had married Mary Brantley on December 15, 1842. On February 28, 1844, she had given birth to their first son, William. Soon after, the

Hoopers moved from the town of Lafayette to a house a mile out in the country.

Hooper apparently found some time for writing during this period, however, and Porter was not to be kept waiting beyond the end of 1844. In December 1844 Johnson J. Hooper more than fulfilled the promise of "Taking the Census" and "A Three Day's Hunt."

Chapter Three

The Suggs Years

Simon Suggs entered the annals of American literature in December 1844 through the pages of the *East Alabamian.* Porter pounced upon the story, retitled it "Captain Suggs of Tallapoosa," and reprinted it in the *Spirit* for January 11, 1845." He lavished praise upon his Alabama correspondent:

It is a great pity that gentlemen of such sterling intellectual ability as the writer of the subjoined sketch should hide their light under a bushel. Our readers may recollect an article published last year, headed *"Taking the Census in Alabama,"* by this same Mr. Hooper, of whom we merely know that he is a young lawyer of repute, and editor, *en amateur,* of "The East Alabamian," published at La Fayette, in that state. His well written editorials are mainly confined to political themes, and it is only once in a long while that he indulges his readers with a sketch like the one annexed—thrown off probably, at a heat. What a correspondent he would make for the "Spirit!" What a "choice spirit" among that circle of "jolly good fellows". . . . (14:547)

"That Circle of 'Jolly Good Fellows' "

By "that circle of 'jolly good fellows,' " Porter meant the far-flung network of gentlemen in a variety of professions who made up the group that has come to be known as "the southwestern humorists." At that time, the "Southwest" included the states of Tennessee, Alabama, Georgia, Mississippi, Louisiana, Missouri, and Arkansas. According to Walter Blair, A. B. Longstreet's *Georgia Scenes* was "the first and most influential book of Southwestern humor. . . ."[1] Although some stories by Longstreet and others had appeared in the *Spirit of the Times* and various newspapers before that, the year of the book's publication, 1835, is a handy one from which to date the birth of southwestern humor in print. Norris Yates notes that, although the *Spirit* first appeared on December 10, 1831, Porter in the early years emphasized sporting news, especially high-stakes horse racing. With the Panic of 1837, however, interest in such racing declined, and Porter gradually increased his emphasis on humorous literature from the Southwest.[2]

To put this year of 1835 into perspective, let us recall that Washington Irving published Knickerbocker's *History of New York* in 1809 and *The Sketch Book* of Geoffrey Crayon, containing "The Legend of Sleepy Hollow," which had quite an influence on southwestern humor, in 1819. The year 1833 saw the publication of Edgar Allan Poe's "MS. Found in a Bottle," Seba Smith's *Life and Writings of Major Jack Downing of Downingville,* and the anonymous *Sketches and Eccentricities of Col. David Crockett of West Tennessee.* In the year 1835 itself—incidentally, the birth year of Samuel Clemens—South Carolinian William Gilmore Simms published his romantic novel *The Yemasee.* Ralph Waldo Emerson's collection of essays *Nature* appeared anonymously in 1836, the year in which Poe married thirteen-year-old Virginia Clemm. The next year witnessed Emerson's *The American Scholar,* Nathaniel Hawthorne's *Twice-Told Tales,* and the graduation of Henry David Thoreau from Harvard.

Just ten years after the publication of *Georgia Scenes,* in 1845, southwestern humor was in full flower, as evidenced by the publication of Hooper's *Some Adventures of Captain Simon Suggs,* Sol Smith's *Theatrical Apprenticeship,* and William Tappan Thompson's *Chronicles of Pineville.* Elsewhere in literary America, Emerson was delivering his *Representative Men* lectures, Poe was publishing *The Raven and Other Poems,* and Thoreau was taking up residence at Walden Pond. In that year Simms, sometimes called "the Southern (James Fenimore) Cooper," published *Helen Halsey; or, The Swamp State of Conelachita,* another in his Border Romances series.

Although the southwestern humorists with their interest in the rustic and the grotesque may be said to have something in common with their more Romantic contemporaries, the southerners Simms and Poe, as well as the Yankees Emerson and Longfellow, their comic realism, sometimes downright earthy, set them apart. Who were these literary pioneers, and why did they blaze a new trail instead of following the broad one worn by their contemporaries?

First, they lived in what is now called "The Old Southwest"; They considered themselves southerners. With a pride bordering on defensiveness, they loved their region and strived to interpret it to readers in other parts of the country. Southerners were conscious of their uniqueness and that of their "peculiar institution," slavery. Not coincidentally, the butt of their jokes was often the traveler, sometimes a foreigner but more commonly a Yankee. In Samuel Clemens's first nationally published piece, for example, "The Dandy Frightening the Squatter" (1852), a steamboat stops at Hannibal, Missouri, and a "spruce young dandy," of unspecified origin, attempts to frighten a "tall, brawny woodsman" by brandishing a bowie knife and two large horse-pistols. The squatter is unimpressed and punches the braggart between the eyes, knocking him into the Mississippi.[3]

Second, they were mostly "professionals" of some kind, most likely lawyers. Among their ranks might also be found an occasional actor, legislator, doctor, soldier, planter, riverboat captain, or painter. Also, in the pattern of Samuel Clemens (Mark Twain), who is sometimes considered the last and greatest of the southwestern humorists, though the only professional writer of the group, they frequently pursued a number of occupations during their lives.

Third, they considered themselves gentlemen, generally Whig gentlemen. This political fact affected considerably the way in which they observed and portrayed their less cultivated neighbors, especially the backwoods specimens, whom many of them regarded as realizations of the darkest fears about the Jacksonian mob.

Finally, they were fairly young, and many were close contemporaries: Joseph M. Field was born in 1810, William Tappan Thompson in 1812, George Washington Harris in 1814, and Hooper, T. B. Thorpe, and Joseph G. Baldwin in 1815. A. B. Longstreet, born in 1790, was the granddaddy of the group, and "Madison Tensas, M.D." (Henry Clay Lewis), born in 1825, the baby. *Spirit* editor Porter himself was born in 1809, and so youthful enthusiasm may be added to the forces inspiring this "circle of 'jolly good fellows,' " many of whom were in their mid-twenties when *Georgia Scenes* first appeared.

The Shifty Man

Pleading lack of space, Porter omitted the following description of the character Hooper had created, an unlikely, unheroic individual about fifty years old:

His head is somewhat large, and thinly covered with coarse, silver-white hair. . . . Beneath these almost shrubless cliffs, a pair of eyes with light-grey pupils and variegated whites, dance and twinkle in an aqueous humor which is constantly distilling from the corners. Lids without lashes complete the optical apparatus of Captain Suggs; and the edges of these, always of a sanguineous hue, glow with a reduplicated brilliancy whenever the Captain has remained a week or so in town, or elsewhere in the immediate vicinity of any of those citizens whom the county court has vested with the important privilege of vending "spirituous liquors in less quantities than one quart." . . . But the mouth of Captain Simon Suggs is his great feature, and measures about four inches horizontally. An ever-present sneer—not all malice, however—draws down the corners, from which radiate many small wrinkles that always testify to the Captain's love of the "filthy weed." A sharp chin monopolizes our friend's bristly, iron-gray beard. All these facial beauties are supported by a long and skinny, but muscular neck, which is inserted after the ordinary fashion in the upper part of a frame, lithe, long and sinewy, and clad in Kentucky jeanes, a trifle worn.[4]

Hooper then goes on to describe the Captain's moral and intellectual character:

His whole ethical system lies snugly in his favourite aphorism "IT IS GOOD TO BE SHIFTY IN A NEW COUNTRY"—which means that it is right and proper that one should live as merrily and as comfortably as possible at the expense of others. . . . (8)
The shifty Captain Suggs is a miracle of shrewdness. He possesses, in an eminent degree, that tact which enables man to detect the *soft spots* in his fellow, and to assimilate himself to whatever company he may fall in with. Besides, he has a quick, ready wit, which has extricated him from many an unpleasant predicament. . . . (8–9)

This latter trait recalls the narrator of "Taking the Census," who admitted that he had escaped drubbings only "by a very peculiar knack we have of 'sliding out' " (150). Manly Wade

Wellman has pointed out physical similarities between Suggs and Hooper himself, quoting a description from the *Alabama Journal* reprinted in the *Spirit* March 23, 1850, in which Hooper is referred to as " 'a kiln-dried specimen of humanity, about 5 feet 10 inches in height,' with a hunched back, picturesquely shabby and untidy clothes, 'foxy' eyes, loose lips and sunken cheeks. 'Hooper is ugly—theoretically, decidedly ugly,' sums up the word picture." Wellman goes on to note that an oil painting of Hooper in the Alabama State Department of Archives and History "strikingly resembles" Felix Darley's drawings of Suggs as they appeared in early editions of *Some Adventures of Captain Simon Suggs* (xviii).

However much Hooper may have drawn upon himself, there was a more direct source for Simon Suggs. Bird H. Young was a friend of George and Johnson J. Hooper. Although he was married with six children and owned a 600-acre farm in Tallapoosa County, Young had been a colorful character in his youth. Legends celebrating his prowess as a practical joker, defrauder of innkeepers, and all-around good fellow persisted for at least a century in Tallapoosa County. Court records of the time attest to his fondness for games of chance, documenting fines for gambling, as well as an acquittal of a charge of "Betting at Faro."[5] Simon himself, it will be seen, was also drawn to the faro box, although never to his profit. In the story "Simon Speculates Again," chapter 6 of the Suggs stories, Hooper goes so far as to state that the Indians called the Captain "The Mad Bird." At one point, Young reportedly threatened to sue Hooper for defamation of character, but reconsidered. Similarly, nothing came of a threat to "flog" Hooper on sight. A jokester himself, Young apparently could also take a joke. A reference to "Mrs. Suggs," though, brought from Young a request that Hooper apologize, and Johnson obliged with a letter in the *Spirit* for November 29, 1845 (15:470).

Other, less direct sources for Simon Suggs include European picaresque literature, the raucous life of the frontier, and, as mentioned earlier, the flourishing oral tradition of tall-tale telling. Scholars agree that Hooper must have been familiar with European picaresque literature and probably drew upon this reading to develop Simon. *Pícaro* is Spanish for "rogue," and Suggs certainly is a rogue of the first order. Such influences are quite general, however, and little more than circumstantial evidence survives to support such assertions.

For further inspiration in the creation of Simon Suggs, Hooper had but to look about him at the uninhibited life of the disappearing frontier he had known since his youth. As Henry Watterson observed in 1883: "The likelihood is that the author in this instance followed the example of other writers of fiction, and drew his hero from many scraps and odd ends of individual character to be encountered at the time in the county towns and upon the rural highways of the South."[6]

Some Adventures of Captain Simon Suggs

Critics have agreed that *Some Adventures of Captain Simon Suggs,* the collected Suggs tales published in 1845, takes the form of a campaign biography, but they disagree as to the extent to which Hooper intended it as a burlesque of campaign biographies. Given Hooper's intense interest in politics, which deepened throughout his life and ultimately overshadowed any purely literary ambitions he might have had, plus the explicit and derogatory references to Andrew Jackson and his biographers that abound in the text, it seems reasonable to agree with critic Robert Hopkins that *Simon Suggs* is "a direct burlesque of political biographies of Andrew Jackson."[7]

The initial three stories or chapters of the Suggs saga appeared first in the *East Alabamian* and then in the *Spirit of the Times.* In the spring of 1845, Suggs stories were reprinted and praised by newspapers ranging from the *Nashville Daily Gazette* and the *New Orleans Picayune* to the Boston *Yankee Blade* and the *Cincinnati Great West.*[8]

Prompted by Hooper's sudden popularity and his own editorial instincts, Porter inserted "How Simon Suggs Raised Jack" into *The Big Bear of Arkansas,* a collection of humorous southwestern stories he was editing for Philadelphia publishers Carey & Hart. So impressed with Hooper's talent was Porter that he urged Carey & Hart to publish a collection of the Alabamian's stories. The publishers' acceptance was immediate, for the *Carey & Hart Record Book,* volume 2, for April–May 1845, shows an entry for the printing of "3000 Simon Suggs."[9] The book was advertised in the *Spirit* as early as April 19, 1845. Its publication was apparently delayed, but Porter printed from proofsheets

"Simon Becomes Captain" in the *Spirit* on May 17, and "Captain Suggs and Lieutenant Snipes 'Court-Martial' Mrs. Haycock" on July 19.

In this same July 19 issue of the *Spirit,* Carey & Hart placed a large advertisement for the first edition of *Some Adventures of Simon Suggs, Late of the Tallapoosa Volunteers: Together with "Taking the Census" and Other Alabama Sketches.* It was scheduled for publication on July 30, but was apparently late, for Porter's review did not appear until September 20. Appropriately the volume was dedicated to Porter, who had already done so much to advance the fame of Johnson J. Hooper—and Captain Simon Suggs.

Enter the Captain

Even though some of the stories appeared in the *Spirit,* they will be considered here as they appeared, as chapters in *Some Adventures of Captain Simon Suggs.* In the first chapter, "Introduction—Simon Plays the 'Snatch' Game," Hooper outlines the biographer's "pious task." He establishes the precedent for such works: "Take, by way of illustration, the case of a candidate for office—for the Presidency we'll say." Explaining the publication of the biography while the Captain is still alive and further establishing a larger political frame of reference for the Suggs stories, he concludes: "Thus, Jackson, Van Buren, Clay, and Polk have each a biography while they live" (4).

In justifying his attempt to describe his own candidate's physique, he refers further to politics of the time:

By this means, all the country has in its mind's eye, an image of a little gentleman with a round, oily face—sleek, bald pate, delicate whiskers, and foxy smile, which they call Martin Van Buren; and future generations of naughty children who will persist in sitting up when they should be a-bed, will be frightened to their cribs by the lithograph of "Major General Andrew Jackson," which their mammas will declare to be a faithful representation of The Evil One—an atrocious slander, by the bye, on the potent, and comparatively well-favoured, prince of the infernal world. (5)

Hooper's deft slurring of the Democrats' bright and shining star and his rather less luminous successor must have delighted the Whig readers of the *Spirit.*

To point up Simon's lack of education, Hooper explains that the artist's portrait in the book is accompanied by "His autograph,—which was only produced unblotted and in orthological correctness, after three several efforts, 'from a rest,' on the counter of Bill Griffin's confectionary. . . ." (Recall that the dispensing of whiskey by the cupful was one of the chief attractions of the frontier confectionery.) He then describes his worthy candidate, Captain Simon Suggs, in the vivid if unappetizing detail quoted above. To complete the characterization, Hooper need only add Simon's motto, "It is good to be shifty in a new country," and we are ready to begin the adventures of Captain Simon Suggs.

Until Simon was seventeen, he lived with his father, a "hard shell" (orthodox) Baptist preacher, in Middle Georgia. One day old Jedediah caught Simon and a Negro boy named Bill playing cards instead of working. As the old man approached, carrying an armful of freshly trimmed hickory switches, Simon pocketed the stakes they had been playing for, telling Bill he would have won anyhow.

The Reverend Suggs soon noticed a playing card, which Simon had been sitting on and had neglected to hide with the rest of the deck. To his father's inquiry, Simon replied that it was the "Jack-a-dimunts," which he had hidden under his leg to play "the first time it come trumps."

> "What's trumps," asked Mr. Suggs, with a view of arriving at the import of the word.
> "Nothin' a'n't trumps *now*," said Simon, who misapprehended his father's meaning—"but *clubs* was, when you come along and busted up the game." (13)

The Reverend at last realized the boys had been "throwing cards" and led them to the mulberry tree for punishment. Simon followed, making faces and threatening gestures behind the old man's back.

The story resumes in Chapter the Second, "Simon Gets a 'Soft Snap' Out of His Daddy." Old Jedediah whipped Simon's black friend, Bill, as the younger Suggs looked on. When his turn came, Simon told his father there was no use in punishing him, because he was going to make his living playing cards no matter what. Failing to sway his wayward son with threats of hellfire, the Reverend Suggs decided to demonstrate the impracticality of supporting oneself by gambling.

Simon had mentioned the game of "cutting Jack," and his father immediately decided he could beat his son at this game, however it might be played. He rationalized away his moral doubts by deciding it would not be betting if he agreed to accept Simon's small bag of silver coins in the certain event the boy failed to cut the Jack. Confident of winning, he readily agreed to let Simon off without a beating and to give him Bunch, the family's half-wild pony, should the boy succeed by some miracle in cutting the Jack.

In spite of Reverend Jedediah's clumsy attempts to stack the deck, Simon unerringly produced the Jack. He then taunted his bemused father, saying that the result was "predestinated," (preordained by God) and "all fixed aforehand."

Chapter the Third, "Simon Speculates," begins the morning after his gambling triumph, as Simon mounted Bunch at dawn and galloped away. He soon became melancholy and reflected sadly that he was leaving his family and friends forever. In a moment, however, he was laughing uproariously as he recalled the load of gunpowder he had put into his mother's pipe before departing and imagined her reaction when she lighted it.

Hooper observes that, as Captain Suggs's biographer, he has no business speculating whether Simon will escape "the clutches of the old gentleman with the cloven hoof" (28). He goes on to explain that the next twenty years of the Captain's life are unaccounted for. He dismisses various rumors and ends by "supposing" that "some enemy of the Captain were to assert" that Suggs had been living in notorious Carroll County, Georgia, stealing horses: "[if any one would say that the Captain had stolen horses] We should say—boldly, haughtily, indignantly say—'LET HIM PROVE IT!' " (30).

The biography of Captain Simon Suggs thus resumes in the year 1833, with an account of the Captain's first "operation" in land speculation. Without a cent to his name, he convinces another would-be speculator that he is about to buy a piece of land out from under the man. In his panic, the man pays Simon $170 and trades his temporarily lame but otherwise sound horse for Simon's nag. As Simon says, any fool could speculate if he had money, but to profit without having a cent in one's pocket requires genius.

Contemplating his killing, Simon reflects that "some fellers" would "milk the cow dry" and hurry to Augusta and enter the land in someone else's name before the once-fleeced victim arrived. He congratulates himself for being above such double-dealing: "Ah yes, *honesty,* HONESTY'S the stake that Simon Suggs will ALLERS tie to! What's a man without his inteegerty?" (37).

Chapter the Fourth is subtitled "Simon Starts Forth to Fight the 'Tiger,' and Falls in with a Candidate Whom He 'Does' to a Cracklin'." Hooper describes the "Tiger," or faro bank, a gambling game. We learn that Simon's only weakness is that he thinks he can beat the Tiger. He never has, but he is sure he will be lucky next time.

On his way by mail coach to Montgomery with $150 from his "speculation" of the previous chapter, he meets a man who is headed there to obtain a bank directorship from the legislature. The man mistakes Simon for a legislator, although Suggs gives him no *direct* encouragement. Before long, the man, hoping to sway the legislator's vote in the matter of the directorship, is paying all the expenses of the "member from Tallapoosa."

The reader can have little sympathy for this victim, whose unprincipled desire for self-advancement leads him to attempt to influence a supposed legislator.

The conclusion of Suggs's encounter with the Tiger is postponed until Chapter the Fifth, "Simon Fights 'The Tiger' and Gets Whipped—But Comes Out Not Much the 'Worse for Wear.'" En route to the gambling casino, he passes a bookstore and delivers himself of two of his characteristic bits of wisdom: "Human natur' and the human family is *my* books, and I've never seed many but what I could hold my own with" and "As old Jedediah used to say, book-larnin' spiles a man ef he's got mother-wit, and if he aint got that, it don't do him no good—" (49–50).

Armed with his mother-wit and the would-be bank director's cash, Simon enters the gambling room. He is ignored, until a young man mistakes him for his uncle, General Witherspoon, the wealthy hog drover. Simon again goes along with a flattering and potentially profitable case of mistaken identity, and the reader is not likely to condemn him, for "Simon thought he discovered a very considerable improvement in the way of politeness on the part of all present. The bare suspicion that he was rich, was sufficient to induce deference and attention" (53). Surely, such people deserve to be fooled.

Simon plays recklessly against his old nemesis and soon has won a pile of markers totaling $1,500. Simon—or rather General Witherspoon—remarks that this beats driving hogs, and the General's young nephew makes himself known. Masterfully, Suggs makes the young man prove that he is indeed the nephew of General Witherspoon. Satisfied at last, the impostor hugs the nephew, bringing tears to the eyes of many bystanders.

Unfortunately for Simon, his luck has cooled during the diversion, and he is soon flat broke, having lost even his original stake. He then proceeds to lose thirty of the General's finest hogs, to borrow $50 from his nephew, and to treat the whole gathering to oysters and champagne.

As he leaves, aware that the real General Witherspoon might arrive at any moment, he bids his "nephew" take care of the cost of the supper and, in a burst of magnanimity, tells him to pick out twenty of the finest Witherspoon hogs for his sister, the boy's mother, as soon as the hogs arrive with the drovers. Suggs then bounces into the mail coach and disappears. This nephew commands the reader's sympathy more than most of the Captain's victims.

Hooper begins Chapter the Sixth, "Simon Speculates Again," with an impassioned denunciation of the dishonest land speculators who cheated the Creek Indians, those "untutored children of the forest" (65). He recounts the tale of a land agent named Eggleston who married a fifteen-year-old Creek maiden in a tribal ceremony. He then talked her father into certifying the land to him, to protect it from "bad white men," and subsequently sold the land and deserted the daughter. When the government soon after transported the Creeks, Eggleston laughed at the Indian's request for a wagon in which he and his pregnant, abandoned daughter could ride to Arkansas.

The Indians naturally afforded business opportunities for that speculator par excellence, Simon Suggs. In this story, an old Indian woman is fond of Simon, as a friend and as a supplier of tobacco and whiskey, and will sell her land to no one else. Although her price to him is only $200, while others have offered a thousand in vain, Suggs cannot raise the money.

At length, he tells the other speculators he is leaving to borrow the money, in Mexican gold coins, from a friend. If he fails, he instructs the "Big Widow" to sell to whomever she pleases.

Just before the appointed time on the next morning, he gallops up dramatically, saddle bags bulging. Instead of buying the land, however, he allows Colonel Bryan, one of the other speculators, to buy out his interest for $500 and the cost of the land to him, Suggs. After receiving the cash, buying the land, and transferring it to Bryan, Simon dumps out the rocks that filled his saddle bags. The speculators vanish.

Simon reflects upon the events and concludes that there is indeed a Providence. He works himself up righteously to the point of declaring that a man who says there is not a Providence has something wrong with his heart, "and *that* man will swindle you, ef he can—CERTIN" (76).

At the start of Chapter the Seventh, "Simon Becomes Captain," Hooper proudly announces that he has reached "the most important period in the history of our hero—his assumption of a military command." Apologizing for his inadequacy to the noble task, Hooper laments: "Would that thy pen, O! Kendall, were ours! Then would thy hero and ours—the nation's Jackson and the country's Suggs—go down to far posterity, equal in fame and honors, as in deeds!" (77). Amos Kendall was Andrew Jackson's biographer. Further, Suggs's heroics are performed during the Creek War, a war that contributed considerably to Jackson's military reputation: "Early in May of the year of grace—and excessive bank issues—1836" (77).

With Whiggish disdain, Hooper describes the conduct of the Jacksonian "mob": "The yeomanry of the country—those to whom, as we are annually told, the nation looks with confidence in all her perils—packed up their carts and wagons and 'incontinently' departed for more peaceful regions!" (78). The yeomanry of Simon's neighborhood have gathered at Taylor's grocery. It is just such a time as cries out for a hero of Simon's mettle, and Suggs, who has brought his family there, is equal to the occasion. He is particularly disposed to be fearless, because he has ascertained that the nearby Indians are not participating in the uprising.

Stationing himself by the whiskey barrel, the better to keep his tumbler full, Suggs speaks eloquently of the need for a steadfast leader in such a dire situation. The assembled settlers agree on Suggs, unanimously, with the exception of one scrawny runt known as "Yaller-legs." The runt, identified as a dirt-eater from North Carolina, observes: "keep close to *him,* and you'll never git hurt." Suggs boots him clear across the room, but he remains in the vicinity, providing comic counterpoint to Suggs's braggadocio. Turning to the business at hand, Suggs asks who would be "capting." A "score and a half masculine voices" shout, "Suggs!" That decides the matter: Simon is now *Captain* Simon Suggs, and the motley group around the whiskey barrel is designated "The Tallapoosy Vollantares."

Comments Hooper: "Thus was formed the nucleus of that renowned band of patriot soldiers, afterwards known as the 'FORTY THIEVES'—a name in the highest degree inappropriate, inasmuch as the company, from the very best evidence we have been able to procure, never had upon its roll, at any time, a greater number of names than *thirty-nine!*" (84). Simon then declares martial law, as did General Jackson in New Orleans in 1815, and he and "Lewtenant Snipes" sit down to drink and play cards.

Sometime later, Captain Suggs has a chance to show his courage and coolness under fire. Outlandishly garbed in her red flannel robe with a cotton handkerchief about her head, the Widow Haycock slips out of the compound to fetch a plug of chewing tobacco from her wagon. Returning, she is challenged by one of Suggs's jumpy sentinels, who mistakes her for an Indian. The guard fires and the widow faints. Simon musters his volunteers and orders a bayonet charge, unhindered by the lack of both enemies and bayonets. The "soldiers" rush out and plunge the ramrods of their rifles into the earth. They discover the widow unconscious on the ground, and Suggs resolves to court-martial her at sunrise for violating the rules of war. He includes Yaller-legs in the charge, too, if they can catch him.

Hooper begins Chapter the Eighth, "Captain Suggs and Lieutenant Snipes 'Court-Martial' Mrs. Haycock," with a mockheroic announcement that Suggs has dubbed Taylor's store "Fort Suggs." For, "Had not Romulus his Rome? Did not the pugnacious son of Philip call his Egyptian military settlement Alexandria?" (90). Lacking the customary drum head, they settle for an empty whiskey barrel. Captain Suggs arrays himself in his full military regalia: blue jeans, frock coat with white cotton fringe, and a large crimson pin cushion on his shoulder for an epaulet. "In lieu of crimson sash, he fastened around his waist a bright-red silk handkerchief, with only a few white spots on it." Mrs. Suggs has stitched two sides of the brim of Simon's beaver hat to the crown and has sewn a saucer-sized red rosette to the left side. Lieutenant Snipes and the rest of the "Tallapoosy Vollantares" are similarly, though not so grandly, decked out, and Hooper has considerable fun describing the antics of the backwoods citizens' militia.

The terrified widow is led in. Her excuse of only leaving the "fort" to get her "tobakker" is taken as a confession, and Suggs immediately condemns her to death by bayonet for violating the rules of war. Hoping Suggs is joking, the Widow Haycock is nevertheless abject and begs for mercy. In due time Captain Suggs does find mercy in his heart. Avowing that he never could bear to see a woman suffer, he lets her off with a $25 fine.

Suggs takes aside the trusty Lieutenant Snipes and gives him one of the dollars, proclaiming: "Simon Suggs never forgits his friends—NEVER! His motter is allers, *Fust* his *country,* and *then* his *friends!*" (103).

In Chapter the Ninth, "The 'Tallapoosy Vollantares' Meet the Enemy," time hangs heavily on the hands of the garrison at Fort Suggs. At length Simon learns of an Indian "play-ball" or lacrosse game in the neighborhood. The Indians being friendly and the games being the subject of spirited betting, he and his volunteers attend. Suggs has bet $10 when one of the white men tells of the Indians' plan to massacre all the whites. The Captain realizes this is a trick to scare away the volunteers and keep their money, so he stations his men by the Indians' ponies. When the signal is given for the supposed massacre, Suggs's men mount up and ride away. Suggs himself escapes with the chief's majestic bay and the shot pouch full of silver wagered on the game.

At the opening of Chapter the Tenth, "The Captain Attends a Camp Meeting," Simon finds himself just as poor following his Creek War heroics as he had been at the conflict's beginning: "Although no 'arbitrary,' 'corrupt,' and 'unprincipled' judge has fined him a thousand dollars for his proclamation of martial

law at Fort Suggs, or the enforcement of its rules in the case
of Mrs. Haycock; yet somehow—the thing is alike inexplicable
to him and to us—the money which he had contrived, by various
shifts to obtain, melted away and was gone for ever" (111).
The $1,000 fine apparently alludes to a similar fine levied by
Judge Dominick A. Hall upon Andrew Jackson for the General's
high-handed administration of martial law in the conquered city
of New Orleans in 1815.[10]

The Captain has no regrets for himself, but he is concerned
for his wife and children. When Mrs. Suggs informs him that
the smoke house is empty and the coffee and sugar are almost
gone, the Captain exclaims: "D——n it! *somebody* must suffer!"
Hooper admits he does not know whether this means the Suggs
family is about to suffer the pangs of hunger or whether some
other party is about to suffer in order that the Suggses be fed.

Shortly thereafter, the Captain arrives at a camp meeting at
nearby Sandy Creek. A tumultuous scene greets him, as numerous people in the hollow are singing, praying, or listening to
sermons dispensed by a half-dozen preachers. "Men and women
rolled about on the ground, or lay sobbing or shouting in promis-
cuous heaps." Hooper attended various churches during his
lifetime, but he was generally considered an Episcopalian and
ultimately became a Roman Catholic. Thus, he is able to maintain
considerable ironic distance between himself and this mass of
black and white worshipers crying out and writhing in the throes
of "the jerks."

Simon Suggs watches the spectacle for a while, noting that
the ministers are most interested in saving the prettiest young
girls, whom they smother with hugs and caresses. Similarly,
he notices that "the women, *they* never flocks around one o'
the old dried-up breethring [ministers]." Simon "viewed the
whole affair as a grand deception—a sort of 'opposition line'
running against his own, and looked on with a sort of professional jealousy" (115).

Presently one of the evangelists notices Simon standing at
the edge of the clearing and immediately recognizes him for
the profligate sinner he is. The Captain permits himself to be
subdued and brought to the front of the congregation, where
he is at length moved by the exhortations of the ministers and
the prayers of the flock to confess his enormous sins. Soon he

is "saved," and "commenced a series of vaultings and tumblings, which 'laid in the shade' all previous performances of the sort at that camp-meeting" (118).

He continues to enthrall everyone with testimony to his salvation and the next morning announces he is going to take up a special collection to build a church in his own neighborhood. Promising to leave the collection in trust with the Reverend Bela Bugg, the chief evangelist, Simon works on the congregation's pride of purse and soon has a sizable sum collected. The Reverend Bugg is eager to lay hands upon the proceeds, but Simon is too shrewd for him: pleading his need to pray over the money even before it is counted, Simon takes it down into the swamp. That happens to be the place his horse is tied, and he rides off, muttering to himself: "Ef them fellers aint done to a cracklin . . . I'll never bet on two pair agin! They're peart at the snap game, theyselves; but they're badly lewed this hitch! Well! Live and let live is a good old motter, and it's my sentiments adzactly!" (126). Hooper has portrayed the ministers, especially the Reverend Bugg, as being so thoroughly corrupt that the reader can scarcely help but applaud Simon for beating them at their own game.

As the title of Chapter the Eleventh explains, "The Captain Is Arraigned Before 'A Jury of His Country'" on the charge of gambling, playing poker. In the course of the trial, Suggs receives a note that moves him to tears. The judge asks the cause, and Simon says his sons are dying. The judge is understandably skeptical, but the note proves to be authentic, from a reputable doctor. The judge therefore dismisses the case so Suggs can go to his sons.

Sometime later, the judge is walking past the local grocery when he sees Suggs regaling his companions with some anecdote. Magisterially, the judge asks Simon why he is not on his way home. Suggs then explains that "these boys here in town" played a trick on him and sent him an old note that Dr. Jourdan had written last summer. So, the note was true, but they tore off the date and delivered it to Suggs. The Captain pretends to be angry at "the boys" for trifling with his feelings, but he and the judge know that the judge is the one who has been had.

"Won't you take some sperrits, Jim?" Suggs offers, but the judge walks wrathfully away.

The final Suggs story in the original edition of *Some Adventures of Captain Simon Suggs* is Chapter the Twelfth, "Conclusion— Autographic Letter from Suggs." Hooper purports to have received from Suggs a letter addressed to "the edditur of the eest Allybammyun, la Fait, chambers Kounty, Al." As may be seen by the misspellings, Hooper misses no chance to demonstrate Simon's lack of education. Indeed, he even professes to have added punctuation. The letter begins:

> Der Johns—Arter my kompliments &c. I set down to rite you a fu lines consarin of them hoss papers (the Captain alludes to the New York Spirit of the Times) you had sent to me from the norrud, which I'm much ableeged for the same, and you kin tell the printer to keep a-sendin as long as he wants to. (134)

This comic misspelling, on which Hooper relies so heavily, would be a mainstay of vernacular humorists well into the twentieth century.

In the letter Suggs comments on the accuracy of Felix Darley's illustrations for the 1845 Carey & Hart edition of *Some Adventures of Simon Suggs.* He chooses one, which came "nigher draggin the bush up by the roots an a most enny thing I ever seed." He tells how he acted as an agent to purchase some slaves and, through his own ingenious logic, managed to come out ahead and still maintain his unjustifiably high opinion of his own integrity. Having dropped a couple of hints about a "muscadine story" which he does not want Hooper to write down, Suggs closes his letter: "Yours, in haist, Simon Suggs!"

His mock-heroic style contrasting vividly with Suggs's semiliterate one, Hooper finishes in the tone of the standard campaign biography, lest we forget that Suggs is running for sheriff:

> Men of Tallapoosa, we have done! Suggs is before you! We have endeavoured to give the prominent events of his life with accuracy and impartiality. If you deem that he has "done the state some service," remember that he seeks the Sheriffalty of your county. He waxes old. He needs an office, the emoluments of which shall be sufficient to enable him to relax his intellectual exertions. His military services;

. . . his gray hairs—all plead for him! Remember him at the polls!
(139–40)

Cynically, Hooper mentions no positive qualifications, only reasons why the voters should take pity on the aging captain and
give him an elected office by way of a pension.

A Writer of the First Rank

Thus the portrait of Simon Suggs was hung in the gallery
of unforgettable American literary characters. A rogue and a
rascal, Simon makes his readers uneasy even as he makes them
laugh. Granted, Simon's opinionated Baptist preacher father,
so smug in his ignorance, deserves to be tricked, but what of
Simon's poor, dear mother, whose pipe the departing prodigal
had filled with gunpowder? Similarly, the dishonest financier
who mistakes Simon for a legislator and unscrupulously attempts
to influence him gets his just deserts, but the Widow Haycock,
whom Simon court-martials at "Fort Suggs," is guilty only of
powerlessness and fear. If we forget ourselves and laugh at
Simon's crueler jests, then the joke is on us.

And yet, in spite of his numerous and ingenious stratagems,
Simon is never on top for long, since it takes only a visit to
the faro bank, the merciless Tiger, to relieve him of all his ill-
gotten gains. Generally, we see Simon up against land speculators and charlatan evangelists, men no better than he. It is in
outwitting the Reverend Bela Bugg and his associates that Simon
is at his best in exposing hypocrisy. Hooper makes it plain that
Suggs and the evangelists are in the same business.

Quick as he is to detect—and exploit—dishonesty in others,
Simon still regards himself as an honest man. After swindling
the land speculator, he knows of a way he could sting the poor
man again but declines to do so. In congratulating himself on
his self-control, he rises to heights of self-righteousness and pro-
nounces piously that "Honesty" is the best policy, "the stake
that Simon Suggs will *Allers* tie to! What's a man without his
inteegerty?" (37). The reader is delighted by this exhibition
of human frailty, by this demonstration that even the most
shameless knave will somehow manage to appear virtuous in
his own eyes.

Just as the quality of *Simon Suggs* established Hooper among the best known of the southwestern humorists, so the stories' technique also marked him as belonging to that school. As mentioned in chapter 2, Hooper's sketch "Taking the Census in Alabama" lacks focus because the narrator's degree of involvement in the action is not clearly defined. In the Suggs stories, however, Hooper makes excellent use of the narrative frame that was such an integral part of the southwestern humorous tradition. According to Walter Blair, the southwestern humorists had numerous models, going back as far as Chaucer's *Canterbury Tales,* Boccaccio's *Decameron,* and the *Arabian Nights.* There were also more modern examples, such as Sir Walter Scott's "Wandering Willie's Tale" from *Red Gauntlet* (1824) or the stories of Maine writer Seba Smith, creator of Major Jack Downing, and the Canadian Thomas Chandler Haliburton, creator of the shrewd New England peddler Sam Slick. Further, oral storytelling was quite popular in the South, and it was natural to present written versions of someone telling a story. Blair lists three types of incongruity resulting from the use of the frame:

(1) Incongruity between the grammatical, highly rhetorical language of the framework on the one hand and, on the other, the ungrammatical racy dialect of the narrator.

(2) Incongruity between the situation at the time the yarn was told and the situation described in the yarn itself. . . . Recounted in the atmosphere of the quiet, peaceful fireside, even the most harrowing episodes of a frontier tale might become comic.

(3) Incongruity between realism—discoverable in the framework wherein the scene and the narrator are realistically portrayed, and fantasy, which enters into the enclosed narrative because the narrator selects details and uses figures of speech, epithets, and verbs which give grotesque coloring.[11]

In *Simon Suggs,* Hooper sets up his frame in the opening paragraph of the first chapter, when he informs the reader of his intention to write a campaign biography:

It is not often that the living worthy furnishes a theme for the biographer's pen. The pious task of commemorating the acts, and depicting the character of the great or good, is generally and properly deferred until they are past blushing, or swearing—constrained to a decorous behaviour by the folds of their cerements. Were it otherwise, who could estimate the pangs of wounded modesty which would result! (3)

Hooper narrates Simon's life story in this highly literate style,[12] but he conveys much of the action in Simon's own backwoods dialect: "Oh, I gin him thunder and lightnin' stewed down to a strong pison, I tell you. I cussed him up one side and down tother, twell thar warn't the bigness of your thumb nail, that warn't *properly* cussed" (43).

The striking contrast between the urbane narrator and his backwoods subjects may further be seen in this description of Suggs's discovery of the Widow Haycock outside "Fort Suggs":

"What's the matter, widder—hurt?" inquired Suggs, raising up one of Mrs. Haycock's huge legs upon his foot, by way of ascertaining how much life was left.

"Only dead—that's all," said the widow as her limb fell heavily upon the ground, with commendable resignation.

"Pshaw!" said Suggs, "you aint bad hurt. Wharabouts did the bullet hit?"

"All over! *only* shot all to pieces! It makes *no* odds tho'—kleen through and through—I'm a goin' mighty fast!" replied the widow, as four stout men raised her from the ground and carried her into the house, where her wounds were demonstrated to consist of a contusion on the bump of philo-progenitiveness, and the loss of a half square inch of the corrugated integument of her left knee. (88–89)

Blair's description of the second type of incongruity resulting from the use of the narrative frame, "Incongruity between the situation at the time the yarn was told and the situation described in the yarn itself . . . ," recalls mid-twentieth-century American humorist James Thurber's definition of humor as "a kind of emotional chaos told about calmly and quietly in retrospect." One place in the Suggs stories where this definition applies is Hooper's comic evocation of the Creek War. It was easy for Hooper and his readers, from the secure vantage point of 1845, to laugh at the panic-stricken Alabama "yeomanry" of 1836.

Hooper makes expert use of the narrative frame in another tale from *Simon Suggs,* "Daddy Biggs' Scrape at Cockerell's Bend." (He had sent it earlier to Porter, who had printed it in the *Spirit* on March 11.) Simon Suggs does not appear in the story, but its central figure and narrator, Daddy Elias Biggs, is funny in his own right.

Hooper explains that "It chanced once, that the writer encamped for a day or two . . . with a company of unsophisticated dwellers of the rough lands . . ." (143). True to the oral tradition, he then turns the narrative over to the chief of these rustic folk, Daddy Biggs, "short, squab, . . . rosy-cheeked, bald, and 'inclining to three-score.' . . ." The story is told in Daddy's own colloquial language, with some asides by Hooper. The author especially notes, with growing astonishment, Daddy's long and frequent pulls on his gallon jug of whiskey.

The story is simple enough, telling how some fishermen from a neighboring, rival region were frightened away when they mistook Daddy Biggs for the Devil. In the best manner of the southwestern humorist, Hooper extracts humor from the contrast between Hooper's erudite language and Daddy Biggs's vernacular. He especially exploits the dissimilarity between the chaos of the tale and the calm of the fireside, another of Blair's characteristics of humorous incongruity. Chaos is contagious, however, and at one point Daddy Biggs talks so convincingly of the Devil that a young listener is frightened into the fire while holding the whiskey jug.

While Blair's third type of incongruity, that between the realism of the framework and the fantasy of the enclosed narrative, applies less to the Suggs stories than to tall tales like T. B. Thorpe's "The Big Bear of Arkansas," there is no question that Hooper's figures of speech are vivid and "give grotesque coloring." In his own narrative, Hooper describes one of the terrified women at "Fort Suggs" as having "face, neck, and bosom crimson as a strutting gobbler's snout . . ." (79).

When Simon accepts the leadership thrust upon him by his fellows in "Simon Becomes Captain," he proclaims boldly: "Let who will run, gentle*men,* Simon Suggs will allers be found sticking thar, like a tick under a cow's belly—" (83). This simile has the comic effect of undercutting the Captain's pretensions, for the tick is hardly an heroic creature. What is more, one would not expect him to call attention to the unflattering similarity between himself and the parasitic tick.

Later, in "The Captain Attends a Camp Meeting," Simon convinces the congregation of his sincerity by personifying Satan as an alligator, which "kept a-comin' and a comin' to'ards me, with his great long jaws a-gapin' open *like a ten-foot pair of tailor's shears—*" (italics mine) (121). At that same camp meeting, Simon "indulg[es] in his favorite style of metaphor" after his "conversion." Poker is more natural to the Captain than religion, but Suggs conveys his message perfectly, exhorting the faithful to "ante up!" and pray, "No matter what sort of hand you've got." As for his own conversion: "Here am *I,* the wickedest and blindest of sinners—has spent my whole life in the service of the devil—has now come in on *narry pair* and won a *pile!"* (italic's Hooper's). For his clinching argument, Simon promises that "Everybody holds four aces, and when you bet, you win!" (122–23).

The seeming inappropriateness of the gambling metaphor to religion has a comic effect. Further, the Captain's figures of speech signal that he has by no means renounced his old ways. And yet, the more we know of the Reverend Bugg and his fellow evangelists the more we realize they are running a racket comparable to a crooked poker game. So we can share Simon's satisfaction as he leaves with the collection money, which Bugg would have stolen anyway: "Ef them fellers aint done to a cracklin, . . . *I*'ll never bet on two pair agin!" (125–26).

Simon's salty aphorisms, beginning with his favorite, "It is good to be shifty in a new country," add further spice to Hooper's linguistic stew. Suggs pays tribute to prudence, "the stob I fasten the grape-vine of *my* cunnoo to" (42). Animal imagery figures in other of the Captain's words of wisdom, as "there is no telling which way luck or a half-broke steer will run" (40) and "it don't take long to curry a short horse" (118).

Also in this volume, Hooper provides healthy doses of the comic realism that gives southwestern humor its vitality and distinguishes it so readily from the genteel romancing practiced by other writers of the time. A squeamish reader might cringe a bit as Simon prepares to share the story of his conversion, "first brushing the tear-drops from his eyes, and giving the end of his nose a preparatory wring with his fingers, to free it of the superabundant moisture" (118).

And there is a strong strain of the primitive humor of physical discomfiture, even of cruelty, running throughout the Suggs stories and other tales. How many modern readers would share Simon's glee as he anticipates his mother's reaction when she lights her pipe, which he has loaded with gunpowder? " 'Now won't it be great!' said he, thinking aloud. 'Won't the old 'oman jump, and sputter, and tear off her cap, and break her spectacles!' and Simon roared with delight at the fun visible to his mind's eye" (26–27). Simon's bullying of the Widow Haycock and his attempts to injure the runt Yaller-legs fit into the same category.

Funnier, perhaps, although still tinged with cruelty, is the scene in "Daddy Biggs' Scrape" when the youth falls into the fire with the whiskey jug. Hooper and another camper cry out for someone to save the boy, but Daddy Biggs has a more urgent concern: " 'Some on ye save the—*jug!*' screamed Daddy Biggs, who was standing horror-stricken at the idea of being left without liquor in the woods" (145).

Favorable reviews from across the nation greeted the volume, and author T. B. Thorpe, editor of the *New Orleans Commercial Times,* lauded *Simon Suggs* not only as humorous writing but also as serious literature. Thorpe declared that Hooper's genius, "if cultivated, would attract lasting attention, and place Mr. Hooper among the first writers of our country." [13] Nationwide enthusiasm for the Captain and his adventures was reflected in sales as well as in editorial adulation, and Carey & Hart printed another 5,000 copies in the fall.

Thus, by late 1845, less than a year after the first Suggs story appeared and scarcely two years after the publication of "Taking the Census," thirty-year-old Johnson J. Hooper found himself a nationally known figure, with readers and editors clamoring for more stories of the wily Captain. One might reasonably expect, as did editor William T. Porter, that Hooper would follow up his advantage and devote most, much, or at least some of his time and energy to humorous literature.

This was not the case, however, even though Porter continued to press him for more stories through the fall and winter of 1845 and reprinted some of the Suggs chapters. In February 1846 Carey & Hart's third edition of *Simon Suggs* was greeted by strong sales and reviews that ranked Hooper with the leading humorists of the day. Neither this success nor Porter's coaxing from the editorial pages of the *Spirit* was sufficient to stimulate Hooper, however, for, sometime in the summer of 1845, he had resigned the editorship of the *East Alabamian* and moved from Lafayette to Wetumpka, where he became editor of the *Whig*. His reasons for moving have been lost, but it may be surmised that he was influenced by Wetumpka's nearness (fifteen miles) to Montgomery, the new state capital. This was to be the first but by no means the last of several decisions in which Hooper placed his political aspirations above his literary ones.

Chapter Four

Chambers—and Other—Gossip

Wetumpka and the *Whig*

Hooper was no stranger to Wetumpka, having for two years practiced law in Chambers County, the circuit court of which was located in his new hometown. He temporarily suspended the practice of law after moving, however, in order to consolidate his editorial position with the *Whig*. A second child, Annie Brantley, named for Mary's sister, whom Johnson had once courted, was born to the Hoopers on November 12, 1845.

As would be his continuing fate in the relationship with Hooper, William T. Porter had to be satisfied with reprinting chapters of *Simon Suggs* and quoting favorable reviews of the book. Editorial queries such as "Why in the world doesn't he write more?"[1] produced few immediate results, although Hooper did write a long letter, to which Porter responded in the *Spirit* for June 13, 1846: "Hooper, the author of 'Simon Suggs,' et cetera, promises to be 'himself again' soon, and we hope to receive something from him equal to his 'Daddy Biggs' Scrape at Cockerell's Bend" ' (16:186).

While the demands of his editorship kept him from humorous writing of any consequence, they did not keep him out of politics. At the December-February 1845–46 session of the Alabama legislature, Engrossing Clerk W. C. Bibb employed Hooper as his assistant for five dollars per diem. The legislature decided during this tumultuous session to move the capital from Tuscaloosa to Montgomery, and Hooper was one of those chosen to inspect the recently constructed state house. While thus occupied, he mailed his political reports back to Wetumpka for the *Whig*.

47

The *Alabama Journal*

Hooper returned home in February 1846, after the legislature adjourned. He was not content to remain there, however. Three months later, he resigned his editorship and took his family to the new capital, Montgomery. There he bought into the *Alabama Journal,* with coowners John C. Bates and E. Sanford Sayre, and assumed an associate editorship. This marked quite a step up, because the staunchly pro-Whig *Alabama Journal* was one of the most influential papers in the state.

The new position represented an advance in Hooper's journalistic career, but it consumed large amounts of time. He was responsible for much of the paper's news and commentary. He also had numerous routine business responsibilities, scouring the state for advertisers and even subscribers. In addition, he purchased paper and other equipment, occasionally utilizing Porter as his agent.

These purchases as well as some personal orders for suits, saddles, and books comprised the bulk of their contact, as once again it was Porter's lot to urge in vain his Alabama correspondent to send more yarns of the Suggs caliber. Although Hooper wrote in December 1846 to request that Porter publish a song that prominent Alabama poet A. B. Meek had dedicated to Mrs. Hooper, he remained silent on the subject of his own literary efforts.

One sample of his journalism does survive, however, "A Snake with Two Heads," which the *Columbus* [Ga.] *Enquirer* reprinted on October 10, 1848, apparently from the pages of the *Alabama Journal.* Hooper professes to have heard this story from Tom Martin, "an old salt, from the Emerald Isle, . . . an Irishman, a painter and *perhaps* the most enthusiastic [Zachary] Taylor man in Alabama. He has travelled much; is full of anecdote, and takes great delight in fretting the assocracy." (The political opponents of Michigan's General Lewis Cass were ever-mindful that his name rhymed with *ass.*)

" 'Ye see, boys,' says Tom, 'ye 'mind of the time I was at the Barbadoes, in the brig Empress. Ye talk about Misther Cass, and, bedad he's for the North *and* the South. He's like the double-headed snake I started to tell ye about." It seems that once Tom and some shipmates were cleaning out the ship's

lockers when they found a bottle of what they thought was
Jamaican rum. They had nearly emptied it before Tom noticed
in the bottom a small, two-headed snake, which the Captain
had preserved to take home as a curiosity. The men rushed
to the side to vomit the "'*snake* sauce' . . . into the harbor
to pisen the fishes." The moral of Tom's—and Johnson's—tale:

"And it's much the same case with ye Cass men; ye're dhrinking
liquor off of a double headed snake; and when, too late, ye find it's
the wrong sort of refrishment, ye'll do as my boys did—come down
to your *kaas,* and throw up the whole of it. So come boys, let's take
a dhrink of geniwine Taylor liquor; and be-Jasus, if there's a snake
in the bottle, ye may sware it's *got but one head;* and that looks to
the SOUTH!"

Written over a dozen years before the Civil War, Hooper's
partisan satire, comical though it is, has in it many of the elements
that would lead southerners to secession. The metaphor of the
two-headed snake and the men drinking the embalming fluid
is repulsive in the extreme. And this contemptuous treatment
of a northern politician, in this case Democrat Lewis Cass, who
attempts to appeal to the South ominously foreshadows the sectional polarization that was already occurring.

If Hooper was deemphasizing literary humor in favor of journalism, he was not neglecting his political career. He attempted
in the fall of 1847 to regain his position as engrossing clerk
for the state legislature. But politics is not a secure profession,
as he was to find, for this time he met with opposition from
the Democrats. The editor of the *Huntsville Democrat* observed
that "there might have been members of the Legislature, who
were aware that J. J. Hooper was sailing, or rather scuttling
under different colors than that of Wetumpka or Montgomery
Whiggery, while he was counting the old lady's chickens in
Tallapoosa county for a Democratic administration." The cham-
pionship of Hooper's mentor, W. C. Bibb, who had hired him
to the position once before, was hardly persuasive to the editors
of the *Democrat,* who opined that neither Bibb nor Hooper
would get a job "higher than that of 'yardsweeper' in the next
Legislature. . . ." [2]

Although the job apparently went to another, Hooper's *Jour-*

nal responsibilities still interfered with his other endeavors. Troubled by ill health during 1848, on January 1, 1849, he left the *Alabama Journal* and the partnership to return to Lafayette. He parted amicably with John C. Bates, who lined him up for a column, "Chambers Gossip," to appear weekly in the *Journal.* Once back in Lafayette and Chambers County, Hooper advertised in the *Journal* that he was resuming the practice of law.[3]

A notice in the Mobile *Register and Journal* for January 13, 1849, suggests how highly esteemed he was in Alabama: "J. J. Hooper has withdrawn from the firm conducting the Alabama Journal. . . . He would be a fine acquisition to any journal which could afford to compensate him for the employment of his whole time."[4]

Chambers Gossip

The January 23, 1849, issue of the *Alabama Journal* featured the first of Hooper's "Chambers Gossip" columns:

To-day, I saw in the Sheriff's custody, two persons charged with offenses of quite a novel character. One of them was a stout old man, familiarly known as "Devil Blackstone," against whom it is alleged that he knocked out the brains of his neighbor's horse, with a sledge hammer. The other was Miss Polly Skipper, in whose possession had been found "a glass pitcher and five tumblers," the property of "Mayflower Division, No. 84, Sons of Temperance." Naughty Polly! . . . to abstract the valuables of a Division with so pretty a name as "Mayflower"! Woman! thou hast no more poetry in thy composition than this name!—Let's see how thou will frisk it, within the cold brick walls, this bitter cold night! . . .[5]

So hungry for humor from the pen of his "Alabama Correspondent" was Porter that he reprinted selections from several of the "Chambers Gossip" columns. Among the earliest of these was "An Alabama Lawyer," which appeared in the *Alabama Journal* on March 5, and then in the *Spirit* on March 24. Porter introduces it as a "side swipe at the legal profession" by the author of "Simon Suggs," himself a lawyer.

In this brief anecdote Judge Stone, the solicitor, and two other gentlemen are examining an applicant for a law license:

"What, sir, is law?" asked the examiner.

"Law,' replied Snub, "is what they do in the court house—suin, and so on."

"Well, sir, what action would you bring against a man who pulled your nose?"

"I'd take him, ex delicto—or—ex contactu—I forget which."

This answer is satisfactory, and the examination continues. *Criminal conversation* is defined as "any bad talk about a man's family." Lest the reader miss the point, Hooper lends the authority of his wit and training to a final judgment on the legal profession in Alabama: "All present acknowledged the ridiculous appositeness of the reply by a shout that awakened father Goodridge from his dreams of horse swaps; and nemine contradicente, Mr. Snub was voted 'learned in the law'" (19:56).

Another vignette of backwoods life is "The Elephant in LaFayette," which recounts the reactions of the citizenry when a small circus comes to town. Hooper attends with his friend Tom Martin, who convinces onlookers that elephants come from Ireland. A man watching the lady lion tamer's bare legs remarks: "I ain't no objection to that woman showin' *her legs* that way; but if Betsy was to—." [6] At this point Betsy comes up and takes her "henpecked" husband away. Here, Hooper is content to let the events speak for themselves.

In a different vein is "Capt. Stick and Toney," a character portrait harking back to Addison and the English *Spectator:* "Old Captain Stick was a remarkably precise old gentleman, and a conscientiously just man." It seems this droll old fellow is in the habit of recording the daily activities of his servants as follows: the omission of a duty incurs a debit of, say, ten "stripes" with the whip, while positive service is a credit of so many stripes. In this anecdote, the lovable codger tallies up the account of Toney, his black "boy of all work," and finds his "balance due" to be fifteen stripes. To make up the fifteen stripe deficit, the ingenious houseboy brings to his master's attention other tasks performed. Irritated, but determined to give Toney *"a few licks any how,"* the Captain arbitrarily assesses the boy ten stripes for "costs."

Toney reflects ruefully: "Bress God, nigger must keep out ob de ole stable, or I'll tell you what, dat *judgmen' for coss* make e back feel mighty warm, for true." [7]

The post–Civil War reader is hard pressed to find the humor in this brutal tale, but, in spite of its eighteenth-century form, it gives some idea of the frequent cruelty of southwestern humor and the violence inherent in the institution of slavery.

A similar character study is "Captain McSpadden: The Irish Gentleman in Purschute of a Schule, Etc." Hooper relies heavily on the Irish stereotype for this tattered, long-winded Irishman, who swaps tall tales about his past for drink and professes to be trying to start a "schule."

He explains to the barkeeper that he lost his previous school because the "little darlints" filled one of his nostrils with snuff while he slept, sending him into spectacular and unprofessional spasms. He then assures a listener that he lost his commission with the Royal Greys because Prince Albert became jealous when the Queen of England took a fancy to him, Captain McSpadden—and all this in spite of his friendship with the "Juke" of Wellington.

Having told his tale—and received his reward in spirits— the Captain nods off, leaving the listener, "Broadbrim," to sum up: "I've hearn tales, and seen liars, . . . and I have hearn of 'stretchin' the blanket,' and 'shootin' with the long bow'; and and I always thought we was great on that, in this here Ameriky, but I find its with liars, as with everything else, *ef you want a extra article you must send to furrin parts.*" [8]

Although these "Chambers Gossip" samples differ among themselves, with some being more like eighteenth-century character descriptions than the more vigorous and modern tradition of the southwestern humorous tale, they have one thing in common: they are inferior to the Suggs stories in humor, vigor, and originality. Nevertheless, Hooper demonstrated that he could still return to the well of inspiration when his editorial duties allowed, for early that year he sent Porter an original story.

"The Muscadine Story"

With "The Muscadine Story," subtitled "The Unwritten Chapter in the Biography of Captain Suggs," Hooper finally rewarded Porter for his patience. The Alabama editor had begun building up the story as early as the concluding chapter of *Some*

Adventures of Captain Simon Suggs, when the "Capting" himself drops a couple of tantalizing hints to "Johns"—and to his readers:

I nevver wus mad, only sed I should be ef you rit that story bout the muscadine vine on the river, which I wouldn't care a dried-apple d——m for *"the boys"* to know it, only the old woman would be shure to hear bout it, and then the yeath *would* shake! Wimmin is a monstus jellus thing.[9]

At the close of the letter, Suggs again beseeches "Johns" to "only be purticler to keep that muscadine story back . . ." (139). Hooper also alludes to "The Muscadine Story" in the introduction to "Daddy Biggs' Scrape."

Hooper begins "The Muscadine Story" by explaining that the passage of time has softened Mrs. Suggs's once-formidable jealousy to the point where she now considers "The Captain's former vagaries—his little peccadilloes—his occasional gallantries—" as "the venial errors of a somewhat extended juvenility" (153). Since the Captain "stands now simply a tottering, whitened, leaky-eyed, garrulous old man," she is merely amused by such tales of his former escapades.

"The Muscadine Story" is a two-part account of Simon's outsmarting of Sheriff Martin Ellis. Spying the Sheriff with a sheaf of official papers in hand, the Captain correctly surmises that he is the person upon whom they are to be served. Before the Sheriff can apprehend him, Simon draws his old revolving pistol and makes a dramatic stand there in front of the courthouse:

"The blood," shouted the Captain, "of the High Sheriff of Tallapoosy County be upon his own head. If he crowds on to me, I give fair warnin' I'll discharge this *revolten'* pistol seven several and distinct times, as nigh into the curl of his forehead, as the natur' of the case will admit." (155)

The Sheriff hesitates a moment, until he recalls that Simon has a "religious dread" of carrying loaded firearms, and the chase is on. Simon is first to reach his pony, and the Sheriff pursues on his bay.

Eventually the Sheriff overtakes his quarry, and the Captain makes a show of giving himself up and strikes a bargain, to boot. Not only will the Sheriff ride fifty yards ahead of his prisoner, but he will also leave for Suggs his black whiskey bottle. (The Captain, who was forced to flee without filling his own jug, is anxious lest the "whole carryvan of blue-nose monkeys and forky-tail snakes" of delirium tremens descend upon him.) Predictably, Simon gives the Sheriff the slip before you can say "bottoms up," and he taunts Ellis as the Sheriff and his long-legged bay flounder about in the swamp.

The story resumes the next day, as Simon sits in an Indian canoe in the Tallapoosa River with Miss Betsy Cockerell, "a bouncing girl, plump, firm, and saucy, with a mischievous rolling eye." The Captain is wooing the young woman, downgrading her other suitors, and describing Mrs. Suggs as being practically on her deathbed: " 'make up your mind to step into her shoes,' he cajoles, 'it looks like it would sort o' reconcile me to lose her'—and here a tear leaked out of each corner of the Captain's eyes" (161).

At that moment the Sheriff suddenly appears, steps from the bank into the canoe, and claims Simon as his prisoner. Simon surrenders without a struggle, and Sheriff Ellis instructs Betsy to paddle them across the river. Ever the philosopher, Simon sighs: "Providence is agin me . . . I'm pulled up with a short jerk, in the middle of my kurreer." Devout believer in the workings of divine Providence though he may be, Simon is never averse to trying to influence the roll of its dice, as he muses: " 'spose a feller tries on his own hook—no harm in takin' *all* the chances—I ain't in jail, *yet!*'" (162).

As luck/Providence would have it, the Sheriff sees bunches of juicy grapes on vines overhanging the river. He attempts to pick some, and so intent upon his tasty prize is he that he pulls himself partway up into the sturdy vines, his feet leaving the canoe for a moment. Seeing this, Simon signals Betsy to use her paddle, and in a twinkling the Sheriff is dangling from the vines over the river, with Simon and Betsy ten feet away. Realizing his mistake, the Sheriff orders Simon to stop his joking. Suggs assures Ellis that he is quite "airnest." The Sheriff begins to plead that he cannot swim.

"Great God," said poor Ellis, "you certainly won't leave me here
to drown—my strength is failing already."

"If I don't," said the Captain, most emphatically, "I wish I may
be landed into a thousand foot h——l," and saying a word to Betsy,
they shot rapidly across the river. (163)

Simon is soon mounted on his pony, and he leaves without
so much as a backward glance at the hapless Sheriff. Characteristically, he sees the workings of Providence in his triumph:

"Never despar," he said to himself, as he jogged along—"never despar! Honesty, a bright watch-out, a hand o' cards in your fingers
and one in your lap, with a little grain of help from Providence,
will always fetch a man through! Never despar! I've been hunted
and tracked and dogged like a cussed wolf, but the Lord has purvided,
and my wust *inimy has tuck a tree!"* (165)

"The Muscadine Story," while entertaining, fails to live up
to its advance billing. Hooper has allowed Mrs. Suggs's jealousy
to diminish, apparently to the point where she could ignore
the Captain's shameless attempt to recruit Miss Betsy to fill the
by-no-means vacant shoes of his wife. There is no hint of any
physical relationship between the Captain and the much younger
woman. (The otherwise frank realism of the southwestern humorists did not often extend to sexual matters.)

The Captain is at his crafty best, however, in outsmarting
his arch rival. And, as noted, he is also in rare form when it
comes to portraying himself as an honest man upon whom divine
Providence shines most deservedly.

The colloquial language is vigorous, too, as the Captain warns
the Sheriff not to try to pursue him into the swamp: ". . . if
you do, you'll have both eyes hangin' on bamboo briers in
goin' a hundred yards . . ." (158). The vivid cruelty of this
figure of speech is reflected in the end of the story itself, when
Simon leaves the Sheriff hanging over the river. Hooper provides nothing to alleviate Ellis's plight, either, as Simon estimates
the depth of the river to be fifteen to twenty-five feet and the
Sheriff begs not to be left there to drown. But, as the literature—
and the court records—of the Southwest attest, those were harsh
times; it often paid to be cruel in a new country.

The *Chambers County Tribune*

During the spring of 1849, while "The Muscadine Story" was being enthusiastically received and reprinted around the country, Johnson J. Hooper's attention was turning to politics. To a brief anecdote titled "A Veritable Mare's Nest," he appended this update on his political fortunes; specifically, he had lost out in a bid for the Chambers County seat in the Alabama legislature:

> I have a little item anent racing that my modesty *almost* forbids me to talk about. This year the whigs of the county determined to select their candidates by voting for them, as at a regular election, and just a week before the thing came off, your correspondent "put his name in the pot." Four were to be nominated for the House— ten on the field—here we go. For some time I didn't know any thing, and when I did come to, found I was a *slow seventh!* Reason—*"too d——d knowin' about Suggs to be honest himself!"* [10]

As an afterthought, Hooper added: "after all, there is but little harm done." Perhaps so, but future events would prove that this was not merely an isolated instance to be laughed off.

"A Veritable Mare's Nest," by the way, was a tongue-in-cheek account of a Whig gentleman who owned a mare mule that had been impregnated by a "stud mule." Mules being sterile, this doubtless amused the *Spirit*'s horsey readership.

In a move typical of Hooper during these years, he abruptly announced in his "Chambers Gossip" column for September 10, 1848, that he would be assuming the editorship of the *LaFayette Sun,* which would be renamed the *Chambers County Tribune.* The paper was to be "Devoted to Politics, Agriculture, and Commercial and General Intelligence." [11] He continued on good terms with his former partner, *Alabama Journal* owner John C. Bates.

The *Chambers County Tribune* proclaimed itself a Taylor paper, supporting recently elected Whig President Zachary Taylor. (Recall Hooper's "A Snake with Two Heads," championing Taylor over Michigan Democrat Lewis Cass.) "Old Rough and Ready" had emerged a hero from the war with Mexico and had not been a Whig long before that party's convention had nominated him on the fourth ballot. A Louisiana slaveholder,

Taylor had alienated the "Northern Conscience" Whigs, although his political principles were rather ill-defined. He had narrowly defeated Cass, with Martin Van Buren of the newly formed Free-Soil party siphoning off some of the popular vote.

Hooper was unable to keep his promise to continue the "Chambers Gossip" column for the *Alabama Journal;* the last one appeared on September 28, 1849. The necessity of filling space in his own paper, however, inspired him to turn out numerous essays and sketches of the sort he had been supplying to the *Journal.* Since few issues of the *Tribune* survive, these pieces are accessible only in the *Spirit* or in Hooper's books, which themselves are rare.[12]

One of the longer sketches, "Jim Wilkins and the Editors," pokes fun at the kind of subscriber editors had to deal with. Set during the "exciting Presidential campaign of 1844," the story tells of two unnamed editors of papers designated by Hooper as the Democratic "Star," supporting James K. Polk, and the Whig "Gazette," which no more "doubted the election of Henry Clay, than it did the shining of the sun, or any other 'fixed' physical fact." [13] Political differences aside, the two editors are good friends and, at the end of every week, "the boys *Pickwicked,* and—shall I tell it? generally got gloriously fuddled together" (97).

At one of these sessions, the two editors have filled their cups with sugared whiskey in the front of a grocery and have retired to the back room for a friendly game of billiards. At this point, Jim Wilkins, "a strong Whig and one of the Gazette's subscribers," enters the front room to buy a drink. He mistakes the sounds of the billiard game for those of a fight, and, from his side of the locked door, cheers on his Whig "Gazette" editor: " 'Stand up to him, my little coon!' shouted Jim—"them's the licks! Hoorow for Henry Clay *of* Kentucky!' " (98–99).

When the "Star" editor calls out, "You'll run out your string before I get another lick," Jim is beside himself lest the Whig lose: "I'll be_____if he ever runs . . . ef he does I'll cut his throat myself. Stand up, my little ring tail, 'tell I git in to you." Jim tries to break down the door to assist, but is restrained by the barkeeper.

Shortly thereafter, the "Gazette" editor exclaims, "I give in—whipped! let's liquor!" (99–100).

Dumbfounded, Jim immediately stops struggling. When the two editors begin to drink together, he steps up to the "Gazette" editor and says, "Stop Jim Wilkins's paper," explaining:

"In the fust and fomost place, you let that feller," pointing to Star, "whip you like a_____! In the second place you hollered like a dog, and then you *treated* to git friends again! . . . I won't read arter no sich a cowardly, no count, sow-pig of an eddytur!" And Jim took himself off in high dudgeon.

The two editors then drank joyously to "The freedom of the Press for ever!" (100–101)

"Jim Wilkins and the Editors" satirizes the rough-and-ready world of the frontier editor, one in which a pistol sometimes came in as handy as a set of type. Henry Watterson wrote later:

In certain regions the duello flourished—one might say became the fashion. Up to the War of Secession, the instance of an editor who had not had a personal encounter, indeed, many encounters, was a rare one. Not a few editors acquired celebrity as "crack shots," gaining more reputation by their guns than by their pens.[14]

Scarcely a dozen years after "Jim Wilkins," a young reporter named Sam Clemens would write in a "Letter from Carson City" in the *Virginia City Territorial Enterprise:*

December 12, 1862
. . .
Col. Williams of the House, who says I mutilate his eloquence, ad-dressed a note to me this morning, to the effect that I had given his constituents wrong impressions concerning him, and nothing but blood would satisfy him. I sent him a turnip on a hand barrow, requesting him to extract from it a sufficient quantity of blood to restore his equilibrium—(which I regarded as a very excellent joke).[15]

Like A. B. Longstreet's "Georgia Theatrics," in which a trav-eler surprises a youth in the woods, practicing his bragging and eye-gouging all alone, just to see how well he "mighta fout," Hooper's tale generates comic relief by suggesting vio-lence that does not actually take place. Some months later, Hooper would write "Jim Bell's Revenge," in which the frontier's potential for violence would be fully realized. "Jim Wilkins" also illustrates—and exaggerates—just how seriously people in the old Southwest took their politics.

Hooper wrote furiously to fill the pages of the *Tribune.* A brief consideration of three pieces written in the late summer and early autumn of 1849, which were reprinted in the *Spirit,* will suggest the flavor of his journalism during this period. "More Silence" recounts a trick played on Jemmy Owen, the "Irish door keeper of the house." On one occasion, when Jemmy had fallen asleep, the Assistant Clerk had startled him into calling for "more silence," to the vast amusement of all.[16] "In a Disagreeable Fix" records how a prisoner in the flea-infested Wetumpka jail pleaded with the touring governor for release from his "disagreeable fix." [17] Porter was happy to copy another bit of editorial filler, "An Editor off his foot," even though he did not yet have the name of Hooper's paper straight:

"An Editor off his foot"—Hooper, the witty editor of the Lafayette (Ala.) Tribune thus gives vent to his bad humor in a recent number of his paper:—
Off our foot—we can't help it, and we wouldn't if we could! For the life of us, we can't make up a decent paper this week. . . . "It's no use knockin' at the door"—we are off our foot, sick, mad, and ready to fight anyone of our subscribers who doesn't like our remarks, provided he doesn't weigh more than one hundred and fifteen pounds.[18]

These sketches, relying as they do on observation rather than invention, lack the structure of the Suggs stories. Nevertheless, added to "An editor off his foot," they paint a colorful picture of a frontier editor's life, a life not far removed from Hooper's.

Johnson also found time to write "The Res Gestae a Poor Joke," which he sent directly to the *Spirit.* Porter printed it in the October 13, 1848, issue. In the time-honored manner of a storyteller passing along a bad joke, Hooper includes in the title a disclaimer, "['We Tell This Tale as 'twas told to us']," and blames the tale on George Woodward.

The unpopular lawyer "Old Col. D." was tricked by two young lawyers into stripping to his shirt and brown wig to swim his horse across what turned out to be a very shallow stream.

In his shirt tail he chased them past a farm house, where a flock of geese frightened his horse. The Colonel was thrown to the ground, and the children gathered around. Soon, the father came out and helped the Colonel remount. The furious old gentleman had not gone a hundred yards when the man called him back. It seems the Colonel had dropped his brown wig.

"Ah, yes," growled D.; "another item in the *res gestae* of this infamous affair."

"What's that you call it—*res jisty?* That's a quar name to me. What do you do with it?"

"My friend, it is one of the set of circumstances all relating to the same infernal rascally trick—"

"You don't take my meanin'—I jist wanted to know what's the name of that *harry* thing in your hand, that I thought you said was a res jisty."

The Colonel attempted to explain *res gestae,* roughly "the body of the case," but ended up donning his wig and leaving in a huff (14:319).

This oral tale, with its contrast between the erudition of the Latin-spouting lawyer and the common sense of the settler, is typical of the sort swapped by judges and lawyers on the "circuit," and is closer than most of Hooper's newspaper sketches to the quality of the Suggs tales.

Simon's Last Hurrah

Porter had to be pleased that this flurry of activity had produced another, the last by Hooper, of the Suggs stories, "The Widow Rugby's Husband." The action takes place at the "Union Hotel," "at the seat of justice of the county of Tallapoosa" (Dadeville).[19] Characteristically—recall Old Kit Kuncker in "Taking the Census"—Hooper finds opportunity to poke fun at opponents of the nullification doctrine of John C. Calhoun and his states' rights supporters: "The house took its name from the complection of the politics of its proprietor; he being a true-hearted Union man, and opposed—as I trust all my readers are—at all points, to the damnable heresy of *nullification"* (166).

Hooper extols the proprietor, one Sumeral Dennis, noting in passing that none of the neighbors was able to trace the family resemblance of the youngest Dennis child, a brown-haired lad in a family of red-heads: "Good people, all, were the Dennises! May a hungry man never fall among worse!" (166).

The politics of the region were strongly pro-Union, and most of the guests at the Union Hotel shared the proprietor's antinullification principles. One of the very staunchest upholders of Sumeral Dennis's point of view is none other than Captain Simon Suggs, "whose deeds of valour and of strategy are not unknown to the public" (167). Unfortunately, the Captain's willingness and/or ability to pay lagged far behind his political zeal, and he had never paid one red cent for numerous stays over the years.

On this particular occasion, Dennis has resolved to listen to his wife and collect the Captain's long-standing debt. As it happens, bad luck is dogging Simon: he has lost all of his money to the "Tiger," the faro box, and the grand jury has indicted him for gambling. Informed by Dennis that his accumulated bill of $31.50 is due, Suggs is so distraught that he calls the innkeeper a "biscuit-headed *nullifier*" when the latter refuses to accept his note. Quick thinking and smooth talking save the Captain from a beating, and he soon talks Dennis into accepting a mortgage on a distant piece of land, worth, Simon solemnly assures his creditor, $1,000. Largely out of party loyalty, Dennis is willing to take the mortgage as payment and throw in his horse, Old Bill. Mrs. Dennis, however, has the last say. She points out quite plausibly that, if Suggs actually had a right to the land, he would not be offering it. And there the matter rests for the night, with the Captain needing to leave town to avoid arrest but being unable to do so until he settles his account with the implacable Mrs. Dennis.

Having drunk three pints of whiskey in a vain attempt to raise his spirits, Suggs is awakened in the middle of the night by a drunken man stumbling down the hall past his room: " 'That thar feller,' said the Captain to himself, 'is the victim of vice! I wonder ef he's got any money?' " (174). The man, who addresses himself as John B. Pullum, stumbles into the room next to the Captain's and continues his drunken, guilt-ridden soliloquy.

Soon the Captain deduces that Pullum has sold some cotton for his wife, Sally Rugby, widow of Tom Rugby, and that he has wasted most of the money on drunken sprees and is afraid to face her. Suggs even interrogates Pullum through the thin partition, and the delirious man answers him.

By morning, Simon has enough information to approach the man aggressively, as he did James, the nephew of General Witherspoon in the earlier story, "Simon Fights the 'Tiger' and Gets Whipped," and put him on the defensive. Poor Pullum is convinced that Suggs must be some old family friend and begs him not to tell his wife or her family of his folly.

The Captain casually mentions that he needs but $50 to "make out a couple of thousand I need to make the last payment on my land." Worried, Pullum begs him not to tell Sally about the sprees: "you don't know how unreasonable she is."

"The devil I don't! She bit this piece out of my face"—here Suggs pointed to a scar on his cheek—"when I had her on my lap, a little girl only five years old. She was always game."

Pullum grew more nervous at this reference to his wife's mettle. (178)

When the desperate man offers to lend Suggs the money in exchange for his silence, Suggs turns him down flat. Pullum begs, and eventually the Captain accepts the $50 "loan," but only if Pullum promises to do better. When Pullum swears he will, Suggs turns on him righteously: " 'No swearin', Sir!" roared Suggs, with a dreadful frown; 'no swearin' in *my* presence!' "

After the contrite husband of the Widow Rugby has left, Suggs pays his own bill out of the $50 and leaves on "his faithful 'Bill.' " As usual, triumph has made him philosophical:

Every day I git more insight into scriptur'. It used to be I couldn't understand the manna in the wilderness, and the ravens feedin' Elishy; now, it's clear to my eyes. Trust in Providence—that's the lick! Here was I in the wilderness, sorely oppressed, and mighty nigh despar. Pullum come to me, like a "raven," in my distress—and a *fat* one at that! Well, as I've *allers* said, Honesty and Providence will never fail to fetch a man out! Jist give me that for a *hand,* and I'll "stand" agin all creation! (180)

This period of intense literary and editorial activity also saw Hooper contributing directly to the *New Orleans Daily Delta* "Dick McCoy's Sketches of His Neighbors," "A Night at the Ugly Man's," and "Col. Hawkins and the Court." "McCoy's Sketches" is Hooper's account of a visit to the "battle-ground of the *Horse-Shoe,* to see if any vestiges remained of *Old Hickory's* great fight with the Indians of the Tallapoosa." [20] His "old crony," Dick McCoy, served as a guide.

Characteristically, the levels of diction are mixed. Some of the language is vivid, for example this homespun simile: "Now and then you may see the cabin of a squatter, stuck to the side of a hill, like a discharged tobacco-quid against a wall." Elsewhere Hooper writes quite formally, describing the natives as "half-agricultural, half-piscatorial." Dick, his "Palinurus" (the Trojan pilot from Vergil's *Aeneid*), is "always *au fait* in regard to matters of settlement gossip."

Dick's "sketches" of his neighbors are tall tales, the first of which concerns Seaborn Brown, who once lay down by the side of the river. So lazy was he that, when it began to rain, he would not get up. The river rose up over him, but, since he was already wet, he still would not stir. His only concession to the rising flood was to tilt his head back to keep the river out of his nose and mouth.

One-eyed Ben Baker, who "weighed two hundred, and was as strong as a yoke of oxen," once became angry at a group of freeloaders and picked them up, one at a time, by the seat of the breeches and "the har of the head" and threw them twenty feet out into the river.

Ben Wallis is the region's *ugly man.* How ugly is he?

The whole livin', breathin' yeth ain't got the match to his picter! His mouth is split every way, and turned wrong-side out, and when he opens it, it's like spreadin' an otter trap to set it. The skin's constant a-pealin' from his nose, and his eyes looks like they was just stuck on to his face with pins! He's got hardly any skin to shet his eyes with, and not a sign of *har* to that little! His years is like a wolf's, and his tongue's a'most allers hangin' out of his mouth! His whole face looks like it was half-roasted! Why, he's obleeged to stay 'bout home; the nabor women is all afraid their babies 'ill be like him. (39–40).

The boat overturns at this juncture, and our narrator and his guide are forced to spend the night with "Old Bill" Wallis, "The Ugly Man" himself.

In the sequel, "A Night at the Ugly Man's," Hooper and McCoy approach the Wallis cabin, which is well kept and surrounded by flowers. They are greeted by Lucy Wallis, the Ugly Man's surprisingly lovely daughter. The Ugly Man himself comes out to greet them, and Hooper adds to his seemingly complete catalog of the Ugly Man's wondrous physiognomy a few savory details such as his face's having "the appearance of a recently healed blister spot" (43–44).

Old Bill realizes at once that Hooper, whose reputation as the census-taker has preceded him, has come to see the Ugly Man. Obligingly, during supper he recounts to his guests how he closes his eyes when he washes, for fear of seeing his own reflection. Even when he was ten years old, he assures them, *"a fly wouldn't light on my face."* Ignoring Mrs. Wallis's protestations that he has made up the story, he tells how, shortly after their marriage, she practiced kissing the cow in order to work up to kissing her husband.

Once, while floating on a flatboat down to Mobile, he picked up a *"level peck of buck-horn-handled knives"* (48) thrown at him by a steamboat crew. (Folklore had it that a horn-handled knife was given to winners of "Ugly Man" contests.[21])

Old Bill concludes with a recent tale of being caught in a hurricane and taking refuge under an oak tree, which was struck by lightning. One of the listeners exclaims:

"Good Heavens! Did *lightning* disfigure your face so?"
"Disfigure h——ll! No. The lightnin' struck right here, as I was sayin', and then—IT GLANCED!" (51)

Hooper has the Ugly Man add a brief Whig note by way of conclusion: "*That* was the main feetur' of old Hickory. He was Ugly some, hisself. God bless him, I've seed him—but he didn't have the gift like me. Good night" (51).

In this tale the reader is overwhelmed by a plethora of exultantly, unabashedly *bad* jokes, of the sort Mark Twain recommended capital punishment for the telling of. Hooper's language is at its picturesque best here, as when he describes Old Bill's mouth as being like an otter trap when opened.

The Ring-Tailed Roarer

The third of those three pieces that appeared in the *New Orleans Daily Delta* in November and December 1849 was "Col. Hawkins and the Court," Hooper's contribution to the "ring-tailed roarer" genre.

Of all the half-real, half-mythical characters who trod the American frontier, none walked with more authority or left a bigger footprint than the ring-tailed roarer. Apparently the real-life models were Mississippi raftsmen or keelboatmen who plied the rivers of the interior in the early nineteenth century. The labor they performed was brutally hard and dangerous, and they demanded no less of their leisure-time pursuits.

One of the earliest printed references to the ring-tailed roarer may be found in Samuel Woodworth's song "The Hunters of Kentucky," commemorating the valor of the Kentucky riflemen who fought with General Jackson at New Orleans:

> Behind it stood our little force,
>   None wished it to be greater,
> For every man was half a horse,
>   And half an alligator.[22]

Soon well-known stage actors were improvising ring-tailed roarers, to great popular approval, and James Kirke Paulding's 1830 play, *The Lion of the West,* was enlivened by James H. Hackett's portrayal of Colonel Nimrod Wildfire. William Bayle Bernard's *The Kentuckian* (1833) and Dr. William Emmons's *Tecumseh* (1836) also featured ring-tailed characters.

Ring-tailed roarers were to be found infrequently in novels: in William Bird's *Nick of the Woods* (1837) and in Emerson Bennett's *Mike Fink a Story of the Ohio* (ca. 1847). The type was most abundantly represented, though, in short tales, some of them drawing on oral lore. Probably the first collection of these was the anonymous *Sketches and Eccentricities of Col. David Crockett of West Tennessee* (1833). Crockett, like Mike Fink and untold others, was an actual person around whom were spun towering tall tales of folk and literary origin. One representative exploit of the Tennessean who was elected to Congress as a Whig in the year 1827 and again in 1833 is a loosely connected series of episodes in which he kills 105 bears in a year.[23]

Johnson J. Hooper's ring-tailed roarer is Col. Hawkins, of "Col. Hawkins and the Court," "the most perfect specimen of the dare-devil frontier-man, that I ever saw, at least in Alabama." Hawkins had once had his skull and brain cloven with a broadaxe and had survived "with all his faculties uninjured." Ever the erudite narrator, Hooper assures us that the Colonel "had cultivated the art of equitation" (horseback riding), and had become a perfect centaur" (102). He delighted in disrupting the circuit courts and would on occasion ride his horse, "Hell," right through a courtroom.

In this story, he barricades himself under the courthouse with food, rocks, and a hunting horn, which he uses to excite all the nearby hunting dogs. When sheriffs come for him, Hawkins throws rocks at them, and the dogs nip them as they bend over to crawl under the building. Soon the judge, an unpopular tyrant, adjourns the court.

Not content with his triumph, the Colonel slips out, mounts his horse, and surprises the judge in the courthouse square. With his hunting horn, he again summons the hounds and with them proceeds to circle the terrifed judge.

Still unsatisfied, Hawkins withdraws, to allow the Sheriff and judge time to gather a posse. He then dons a whiskey barrel for armor and charges into the posse, accompanied by his canine volunteers. The judge, mounted on a pony, scatters with the rest, but the implacable Hawkins chooses him out and chases him into a tan yard, where his pony pitches him into a "not inodorous vat." Pausing to toss the barrel through a grocery-store window—and onto the grocer's head—Col. Hawkins, "whooping at the top of his voice, rode furiously out of town" (108).

Col. Hawkins the ring-tailed roarer is in some ways a more typical figure of southwestern humor than is Simon Suggs. Even if the reader agrees that the tyrannical judge deserved the treatment he received, the grocer was merely an innocent bystander. Simon rarely inflicts so much physical discomfort.

In contrast, George Washington Harris's Sut Lovingood wreaks painful havoc indiscriminately. In "Sicily Burns' Wedding," Sut chances upon the wedding celebration of an ex–girl friend. Not having been invited, Sut is (characteristically) on the outside looking for a chance to cause mischief, and soon finds a way: he slips a basket over the head of Sicily's father's bull. The panic-stricken brute begins to back up and overturns a beehive. In the resulting chaos, the wedding is disrupted, the house is wrecked, and the guests are severely stung. Understandably, the jilted Sut teases Sicily about enjoying a "new sensation," but, the next day, he taunts other guests who are painfully swollen from stings.[24] It is in Col. Hawkins, more than in Simon Suggs, that Johnson J. Hooper captures this swaggering cruelty so characteristic of southwestern humor.

"Jim Bell's Revenge"

Much of the cruelty absent from Hooper's other writing seems to have been distilled and poured into "Jim Bell's Revenge," alternately titled "Fun on the Circuit," which appeared in the *Spirit* for July 6, 1850, by way of the (Boston) *Yankee Blade.* Written perhaps a year after "Colonel Hawkins and the Court," "Jim Bell's Revenge" retells "an amusing scene on the public square," which Hooper, at that time a state solicitor, witnessed in one of the county-seat towns:

The court house town of Randolph, like other villages, had its dozens of wild youngsters—clerks, overgrown school-boys, and other larks, who were always ready for any deviltry that might turn up. Of course, they acted in concert—I never knew a set of the kind that did not. The thing is a sort of free masonry of mischief, and the members are usually all "bright." Let one make a demonstration against any luckless individual selected as a victim, and upon the instant, the whole clan take the cue, and begin the work of tormenting. Generally some inebriate is chosen, and while Bill Swinney holds him in conversation, Tom Abels slips up behind, and lets fly into his ear a cold stream of water from a squirt—or Tom Owen, pretending to brush an insect from his hair, "embraces the opportunity" to smear the unfortunate's face with a "good article" of boot blacking (71).

Years later, Samuel Clemens would paint a portrait of a similar group in *The Adventures of Huckleberry Finn* when describing a "little one-horse town" in Arkansas:

There was empty drygoods boxes under the awnings, and loafers roosting on them all day long, whittling them with their Barlow knives;

and chawing tobacco, and gaping and yawning and stretching—a
mighty ornery lot. They generly had on yellow straw hats most as
wide as an umbrella, but didn't wear no coats nor waistcoats; they
called one another Bill, and Buck, and Hank, and Joe, and Andy,
and talked lazy and drawly, and used considerable many cuss-words.
There was as many as one loafer leaning up against every awning-
post, and he most always had his hands in his britches pockets, except
when he fetched them out to lend a chaw of tobacco or scratch.[25]

In Hooper's anecdote, "the boys" stir up a fight between
Ephraim Biddle and Jim Bell, neither of whom knows the other,
and neither of whom is young. Jim's deafness adds to the confusion. Eventually the boys get the two drunken victims into a
darkened cellar to fight it out.

Sometime later, Jim Bell, his hand wrapped in a handkerchief,
comes to Solicitor Hooper to press charges against himself and
Ephraim Biddle for an "affray," under which charge damages
might be found against both defendants. He does not want to
file charges of assault and battery, because they both agreed
to fight. Jim's grievance stems from the fact that during the
struggle Eph got Jim's thumb in his mouth and began to chew
it. Hailing from Georgia, which was known for eye-gouging,
Jim began ". . . to sarch for a soft spot in his head with my
other thumb, and sure enough, it slipped into his right eye,
and so I give it the *Georgy set, and then brought a raunch and
commenced feelin' for the strings"* (79).

Try as he might, poor Jim could not gouge out that eye,
and he could not reach the other one. Eventually he had to
holler quits, for the boys to let them out. In the light, Jim
realized what a foul trick Eph had played: "You see whar I
was a gougin', *thar warn't no eye,* nor hadn't been for many a
day—*it was gouged out ten years ago, in Georgy!* So, 'Squire, I
want the law run agin us both, and I'll see ef the one-eyed
rascal can play any advantages in *that* game" (79).

The modern reader may not find much to laugh about here,
but the sketch gives a good idea of the brutality of the frontier,
the same brutality Clemens recorded in continuing the description of the Arkansas town begun above:

You'd see a muddy sow and a litter of pigs come lazying along the
street and whollop herself right down in the way. . . . And pretty

soon you'd hear a loafer sing out, "Hi! *so* boy! sick him, Tige!" and away the sow would go, squealing most horrible, with a dog or two swinging to each ear, and three or four dozen more acoming; and then you would see all the loafers get up and watch the thing out of sight, and laugh at the fun and look grateful for the noise. Then they'd settle back again till there was a dog-fight. There couldn't anything wake them up all over, and make them happy all over, like a dog-fight—unless it might be putting turpentine on a stray dog and setting fire to him, or tying a tin pan to his tail and see him run himself to death.[26]

This catalog of cruelty to animals is but a prelude to a scene in which Boggs, the town drunk, insults Col. Sherburn, the town aristocrat. Sherburn shoots Boggs, "the best-naturedest old fool in Arkansaw," in cold blood right there in the street. The loafers and other citizens threaten to lynch the Colonel, but lack the courage to do so. Clemens, however, was doing more than merely recounting an "amusing scene," and had the Colonel deliver a scathing speech on the theme "the average man's a coward," demonstrating just how far beyond the southwestern humorous tale Clemens had gone.

The Bloody Ninth

To capitalize further on this period of literary productivity, Hooper arranged to have a number of the pieces published by Tuscaloosa printer M. D. J. Slade under the title *A Ride with Old Kit Kuncker and Other Sketches.* And, in the midst of this publishing activity, came Johnson J. Hooper's first major political venture: in October 1848 he announced that he was running for the solicitorship of the Ninth Circuit, the candidates to be voted on by the two houses of the state legislature.

While Johnson was preparing material for publication and running against four opponents, a second son, Adolphus Stanford, was born to the Hoopers on October 29, 1849. (Daughter Annie Brantley Hooper had died in the summer of 1847, before her second birthday.) In other family developments, Hooper's father, Archibald, and his mother, Charlotte, moved sometime during that year from his daughter's home in Philadelphia to Crawford, Georgia, to live with Johnson's older brother, George. Johnson occasionally visited his parents there.

Concerning the election, Hooper wrote to his brother-in-law, Alsea K. Brantley, that he would be joining him in Arkansas should he lose. This migration was not necessary, however, for Hooper easily won the right to ride the circuit as the State of Alabama's prosecutor for $1,500 per year plus certain allotted fees. Two of his vanquished opponents were quite formidable and went on to become successful later in life: Alexander W. Bowie as an Alabama judge and state legislator and Milton S. Latham as a United States senator from California. Latham, according to William Garrett, gave as his reason for leaving that "he would not live in a state where Johnson Hooper could defeat him for solicitor." [27]

As its nickname indicates, law and order had made scant inroads into the Bloody Ninth, which consisted of Chambers, Talladega, Russell, Macon, Randolph, and Tallapoosa counties. Just a few years before, it had been Muscogee Indian territory, and some of the white inhabitants were scarcely more "civilized" than the Indians they had displaced. The state's prosecutor must have had a busy time, for, as court records indicate, there were numerous cases of arson, burglary, murder, adultery, gambling, and, especially, assault and battery and assault with attempt to murder. The fact that many of the judges themselves were fond of drinking and card-playing had in the past inclined them toward leniency. Hooper rode the circuit, six counties and 160 miles,[28] on horseback. According to Marion Kelley, when in Dadeville Johnson lived in the Dennis Hotel, the original of the "Union Hotel," setting for "The Widow Rugby's Husband."

His story "The Bailiff That 'Stuck to His Oath' " gives some idea of what the fledgling solicitor faced on the circuit. Describing the early days of his solicitorship as "a rough road to travel," Hooper quotes Bill Swallow, his predecessor, as declaring "that the solicitorship of the Ninth would starve any man that hadn't luck and skill enough to beat the bench, bar, and juries of the circuit, at Poker" (65).

Hooper himself is the butt of the joke played by a bailiff on the inexperienced state's attorney. When Hooper entered the courthouse, the bailiff denied him access to the grand jury. Hooper ranted and fumed, but the bailiff stood fast, citing his oath as a sworn officer not to speak to the jury or allow anyone else to do so. Finally, Hooper backed down and "slunk off to [his] room." Later, after the foreman of the jury had given him the proper instructions, the bailiff apologized profusely to Hooper and allowed him to see the jury.

Hooper was at first uncertain as to whether the bailiff had been in earnest or had merely been playing a joke on a greenhorn. His doubts were removed, however, when that night he passed a "grocery" and heard his bailiff telling over a cup of whiskey how he had fooled the new solicitor and prevented him from surprising the grand jury in the midst of a poker game. The "boys" had a hearty laugh, and Hooper hurried away, vowing vengeance. We have no record of any such vengeance ever being realized.

A Ride with Old Kit Kuncker

Not long after Hooper's election victory, in December 1849, *A Ride with Old Kit Kuncker* appeared. Johnson dedicated the book to his friend Alexander B. Meek, Alabama's leading poet. He was returning a favor, for in 1846 Meek had inscribed his song "The Rose of Alabama" to Mrs. J. J. Hooper. In addition to the title story, the slender volume included several stories, most of which originally appeared in the *Alabama Journal* and/or the *Spirit of the Times.* The best of these were "The Muscadine Story" and "The Widow Rugby's Husband."

Titled " 'Taking the Census.'—Part III, From 'A Ride with Old Kit Kuncker, and other sketches.; BY J. J. HOOPER, AUTHOR OF 'SIMON SUGGS,' ETC.' " the story was reprinted in the *Spirit of the Times* for March 16, 1850 (41), beginning with a reminder that in "Taking the Census," "we" had promised "our old friend," Kit Kuncker, that we would visit him and meet Jim Kent, whose sister, Becky, "was so ugly 'that the flies wouldn't light on her face.' "

Old Kit has another story to tell: "You see, 'squire, me and my Jim was a haulin' a load of whiskey up from Wetumpky, in the spring of '36. . . ." They met an unsuspecting traveler with a fine horse, "just rizin' four year old, fat, *and hilt his head like the Queen of Sheby.*" Old Kit and his son played on the Yankee's fears of Indians and soon talked him into trading his steed for their hard-gaited horse, Old Cuss, which they said would be just the horse to take him to safety. "We made the trade mighty quick, for he had the injun ager [fever] 'twell his eyes was big as sassers!" Soon the ignorant Yankee was on his way, buttons rattling from the nag's stiff gait. A war whoop from Jim sped them along.

When this tale is finished, Hooper and Old Kit arrive at the shanty of Jim Blake, one of those settlers whom Uncle Kit had brought up from Georgia in his wagon some years ago. Jim is in no mood to have his "sensis" taken, and curses the census-taker and Democratic President Martin Van Buren, as well. Though Kit says that Old Hickory picked Van Buren and therefore he will do, Jim announces his intention to vote for Harrison.

Distressed that a boy he has "raised" has turned out to be a Nullifier, Kit confides after they leave: "*A little more and he'd a cussed Old Hickory!* and ef he had, by the God that made me, I'd a tore his liver out!"

Eventually they reach the residence of Jim Kent, brother of Becky Kent, the ugly spinster mentioned earlier. She is not at home, but as soon as they leave, Old Kit tells a story on her.

It seems that some time ago he came upon "scrawny Becky Kent, settin' on a bag o'corn, on her old blind horse, and him a standin' stock-still in the middle of the ford." Somehow, she had dropped the horse's bridle, the bag of corn had shifted, and she had grabbed it, leaving her to hang down on one side of the horse, "her face . . . as red as a gobbler's snout," holding onto the bag of corn, which balanced her on the other side of the horse. If she were to let go, she would fall into the river. Uncle Kit intended to help her, but he had to have his fun, first. Becky was a heavy snuff user, but she had always denied it.

At last, I seen an old mustard bottle stickin' out from her bosom, and ses I, Miss Becky will you give your uncle Kit a pinch of snuff? Ses she, help me, for the Lord's sake—I'm mighty nigh gin out— and 'squire, she *was* on a *temenjus* strain! but I tho't I'd plague her some, and after cuttin' of some shines, I made a motion to snatch at the bottle o' snuff!—She gin a little jerk back!—the *big eend* got a start!—still she hilt her grip with both hands!—and the next thing, *somethin' riz in the air, like a small cloud of calico and dry corn stalks!*

and the durndest *ca-slosh* on t' other side of the horse, that ever you
heerd! *A—waugh! What sloshin'.*
    Hooraw, Becky! rise gall! I was lookin' t' other way! ses I, *for I
knowed she was 'shamed!* I laughed, however, and she mighty nigh
cussed!

Kit laughs as he tells how Becky never forgave him.
    Soon they have finished taking the census of Old Kit's Union
Crick settlement and arrive back at his house.

As Uncle Kit threw down our saddles in his porch, said he: "I didn't
tell you 'squire to-day about how old Henry Teel larnt to make soap
out'n *sal sody,* and how he sold the reseet to old Mrs. Spraggins,
and what a devil of a paddlin' the old woman gin him with the battlin'
stick when she found the soap would shrink,—did I? Well come in
and we'll take a sip of *branch-water,* and I'll norrate it to you. . . .
Walk in 'squire, and take a seat in yer old Union Uncle's house!

    While "A Ride with Old Kit Kuncker" is humorous, it relies
heavily on the character of Old Kit, which Hooper had created
ten years earlier. Repetition of such phrases as "so ugly flies
wouldn't light on her face," used in "A Night at the Ugly
Man's," and "red as a gobbler's snout," from "Simon Becomes
Captain," suggests a flagging of his powers of invention.
    Of the sketches and stories included in *A Ride with Old Kit
Kuncker* but not previously discussed here, two present comic
Irishmen: In "An Involuntary Member of the Temperance Society," Hooper and a friend give a wagon ride to a tall-talking
Irishman who claims to be a member of the Temperance Society.
When a flask of whiskey is passed, however, he is the first to
reach for it, explaining that he was *technically* a member once,
because his employer paid only once a week, and so for part
of the week he was an *"involunthary mimber"* of the Temperance
Society (133–136). "Jemmy Owen on the Senatorial Election"
lightly recounts the efforts of the state senate's Irish doorkeeper
to avoid endorsing either of two candidates in a senate election
(156–59).
    "An Alligator Story" presents a Yankee as the butt of a joke,
telling how a "gentleman from some one of the Northern States"
was traveling up the river from Mobile to settle in Selma. The
Yankee asked "Tom Judge, of Lowndes—I think it was Tom—

" if there were any alligators in the river. Tom said, "not now!" This reminded him of his friend who died the year the alligators disappeared from the river.

The "green 'un" asked: "Was your friend drowned?" and is told that the friend died of the congestive fever, the most dreaded of southern diseases. After a pause, Spooney assayed again: "What caused the disappearance of the alligators?" *"They died of the same disease."* The Yankee did not get off the boat, but returned to "more salubrious regions!" (140–41). The modern reader, whether Rebel or Yankee, is not likely to split his sides laughing over this one, but it was reprinted in William E. Burton's 1858 *Cyclopedia of Wit and Humor.*[29]

Two of the pieces, both apparently written especially for this volume, are essays on character types, in the eighteenth-century manner. "Our Granny" is an affectionately condescending essay on grandmothers in general, and "our" Granny Mitchum in particular. In "The Good Muggins," Hooper defines his aim as to "chalk down a rough outline of an individual, to represent a growing class—a recent species of the genus 'Loafer.' " The loafer, the "good Muggins," is "apt to be a subscriber to some leading political journal—until his name is stricken from the list for non-payment" (151–55).

The final two selections are slight: "A Legislative Election" tells of a candidate for legislative clerk who claimed he lost an election because he made a good impression on the legislators, but they somehow knew him by the other candidate's name and voted accordingly (137–39). "Montgomery Characters," reputedly copied from the *Chambers Tribune,* presents three flattering character sketches: "The Grand Secretary," "Ned H——k," and "The Colonel." Ned H——k is apparently Edward, "Horseshoe Ned," Hanrick, a close friend of Johnson's. Writes Hooper: "A jolly old cock is Ned. No one lives more happily or harmlessly, than he" (160–69).

A Ride with Old Kit Kuncker was well received critically, at least in traditionally friendly corners. The ever-faithful Porter reprinted several of the stories and advised readers to order the volume by mail. The *Alabama Journal* loyally praised the book as embracing "within its covers as much hearty, genuine humor as would have made the reputation of a dozen sketch-writers. . . . Hooper's writings have been read with delight by thousands of the purest and most cultivated intellects of the land." Bouquets were not forthcoming from every quarter, for the *Journal* felt obliged to reply to the *Mobile Tribune's* charge that Hooper had used inelegant language:

Hooper, in the language which he puts occasionally in the mouths of some of his characters, may have been more faithful to nature than many approve—perhaps, in some instances, to a fault; but these are minor defects which do not dim the acknowledged and transcendent merits of most of the descriptions . . . we know of no writer with more ability to draw deeply and use effectually from the "pure well of English undefiled." [30]

A. Hart of Philadelphia published an expanded edition two years later, in 1851, as *The Widow Rugby's Husband, A Night at the Ugly Man's and Other Tales of Alabama,* changing the order of the stories and adding four.

Riding High

In the spirit of good-natured joshing that so often characterized editorial exchanges of the time, Porter reprinted from the *Alabama Journal* of February 26, 1850, by way of the *Augusta* [Georgia] *Republic* a description of Hooper signed by "Big Ugly." The sketch apparently had Hooper's prepublication approval, and there is even some suspicion that he might have written it himself.[31]

A kiln-dried specimen of humanity, about 5 feet 10 inches in height; a cross between an Egyptian mummy and a shriveled pumpkin, conveys to the mind a faint idea of Johnse. . . .
An old silk which has honestly worn, and boldly wears the title of "a shocking bad hat," covers a small bullet-shaped head; a sack coat of grey tweeds covers, while it displays to perfection, a hump which would excite the envy of an Eastern dromedary, or Parisian belle; a striped vest buttoned closely to the throat, hides a shirt with which the washerwoman has but a slight acquaintance; breeches, whose original color is "questio vexata," encase a pair of legs formed in humble imitation of the Jack of diamonds—below the termination of the breeches are a pair of pigeon-toed feet, covered with yarn socks, one of which is always worn wrong side outwards, and a pair

of kip brogans, as unconscious of blacking, as their owner's face is of soap.

Hooper's face can "better be imagined than described." In attempting to take his Daguerreotype, Park has broken two cameras! . . . His hair is a sun burnt brown, seldom combed, never oiled; his forehead is bold and intellectual, it is the sole mark by which you recognize his face as human; his eyes are foxy . . . his lips, full and sensual, show little firmness, but much ambia; his nose a counterpart of those we daily see attached to the denizens of that portion of Montgomery known as Jerusalem; his cheekbones are strongly defined, and his cheeks sunken. . . .

. . . Hooper is ugly simply because he can't help it. From self defense, he has cultivated a bold and original style, with a fine appreciation of the ridiculous. . . . But we must say that he pursues his foes with as much zeal as he serves his friends, be the injury great or small, the punishment is in full. He never forgets an offence, and never forgives one.

"Big Ugly" [32]

In addition to providing a verbal caricature of Hooper's physical features, "Big Ugly" shows us in this last sentence a different Johnson J. Hooper, the political warrior whose toughness would be tested in the partisan strife to come.

About a year later Porter reprinted "Shifting the Responsibility—A Hard Shell Story" in the *Spirit* for April 5, 1851. Although the story was unsigned originally and again when it appeared in *Yankee Notions, or Whittlings from Jonathan's Jack-Knife* 6 (April 1857):125, there has never been any question that Hooper wrote it. The brief story, prefaced as being told to Hooper by "A friend who is fond of a good joke," concerns Brother Crump and Brother Noel, close friends and members of the same church. One year Brother Crump invested some of the proceeds from his cotton crop in a barrel of whiskey. His steady progress in consuming said barrel drew the attention of the whole settlement, and in due time Brother Noel came calling on his friend. Delicately, he broached the subject of Brother Crump's drinking. Brother Crump admitted the problem had worried him:

"So I left it to the Lord to say whether I was going too far in sperits. I put the whole 'sponsibility on Him; I prayed to Him ef I was drinkin' too much, to take away my appetite for sperits." [When the Lord didn't take away his thirst, Brother Crump concluded he was] "clear of the 'sponsibility, any way."

"The Lord's will be done!" ejaculated Noel, and after taking another dram, he went home, thinking all the way how cleverly Brother Crump had shifted the responsibility.

This sort of fun at the expense of the pious would come back to haunt Hooper in later years.

Enjoying his prestige, popularity, and even a little prosperity (he had joined the Masons on October 31, 1851), Hooper began to find time and resources for hunting, ordering guns and a bird dog through his friend Porter. Later, in a piece dated "East Alabama, July 2, 1853," he informed Porter that, "if it pleased you," he would be furnishing "such notes of birds, beast, and men, in this region, as might seem worthy of preservation" (*Spirit* 23 [July 16, 1853]:254). Cryptically he signed the letter "NUMBER EIGHT."

Newspapers of the time suggest that Hooper was in some political trouble, as the *Macon Republican* charged him on June 30, 1853, with straddling the fence, with "one eye towards Montgomery, and one towards Chambers." [33] Even Hooper's old friend and former editorial associate, J. C. Bates, hinted at the prevailing uncertainty as to Hooper's political convictions in this otherwise friendly notice in the *Alabama Journal* for November 12, 1853:

We had the pleasure of seeing for several days our old friend and "fides Hooper of the Bloody 9th." He was in tolerable health though somewhat worn by the fatigues of the circuit. *Though we have not been able exactly of late years to trace our old confrere's position in politics* [italics mine], we know him to be the same, genuine hearted—unchanged and unchangeable as ever. [34]

Also during this period he wrote for Porter some of the promised "notes of birds, beasts and men," from "down 'pon de branch." The earliest of these, "An Otter Story,—Game—ETC." (*Spirit* 23 [August 6, 1853]:291), dated "East Alabama, July 17, 1853," is undistinguished.

Another of the notes, "Daddy Donk's Sermon at Timber-Gut," (*Spirit* 23 [September 3, 1853]:337), is representative

of Hooper at his best. After mentioning his August 15 quail
hunt, he refers to Parson "Daddy" Donk, to whom he had
alluded in "An Otter Story," and gives the text of a sermon
by "Father Donk, of the 'Two-Seed Divines.'" Daddy Donk
is an anti-Temperance preacher who answered his critics as follows: *"Satan has had another flirt with the old strumpet of Babylon—*
and what d'ye reckon, she's brought forth? Why, SONS-O'-TEM-
PERANCE."

Lest these sons move in on Timber-Gut, he reviewed how
the congregation built its church:

"And the Lord prospered the church on Timber-Gut, on every hand;
and we took the money that was over and above the buildin' of the
meetin' house, and we laid it out in *fifteen gallons of mighty good corn
whiskey,* for the breethren to use on meetin' days! Oh Glory to the
Lord, *them* was the days when the church on Timber-Gut was like a
green bay tree! *Then* you might a seed the breethren a flockin' in
of a Sunday mornin'! *Then* was the time your old Daddy Donk went
down into the water [for baptism], with somebody or another, every
meetin' day! And Breethren"—here the speaker sobbed between his
words—"There was added to the Church *ondurin' the time we had
that good sperrits, forty-five members!*

"Praise God! it was just adzactly THREE TO THE GALLON, BREETH-
REN!"

He pointed out that Satan began to gain an advantage when
the liquor ran out. At the conclusion of his moving sermon,
the congregation immediately raised the funds "to procure a
suitable supply of munitions" for the war on Satan.

Displaying the vigor and vividness of the Hooper of old,
Johnson recaptures perfectly the cadence of evangelical ha-
rangue. Daddy Donk is a combination of the Reverend Bella
Bugg and Simon Suggs himself, warning of the rising tide of
the Temperance heresy: "Here I've striv and here I've rastled,
and here I've snake-poled Satan as far as the Lord has give
me strength. Praise the Lord, I've give the old varmint's hide
some mighty tight dressin's, but he's a gittin' the upper hand
of old Daddy Donk now." And the utter incongruity of calculat-
ing the ratio of new members to gallons of whiskey consumed
is vintage Hooper.

The next month found Porter reprinting another of Hooper's

sketches, "Quail in Alabama" (*Spirit* 23 [October 1, 1853]:390), dated "East Alabama, Sept. 18, 1853," again over the as-yet-unexplained pseudonym, "NUMBER EIGHT." The title is derived from a light account of how Hooper shot a bird he thinks might have been a snipe. In mid-piece, however, he breaks off and shows an unaccustomed side to jolly, fun-loving Jonce:

> Since I commenced the writing of this letter I have been looking over the yellow fever accounts from Mobile; and really I have no heart to continue in a strain of gossiping levity. There are noble hearts there ceasing to beat, every day, and panic and want are making even life frightful. Already I see loved and familiar names on the dark catalogues of the dead, and God only knows when and how it will end. The weather is now, and has been for days past, unusually warm and unseasonable; the atmosphere constantly humid. An early frost—though it shortened the cotton crop a million of bales—would be the richest of God's blessings.
>
> Always yours,
> NUMBER EIGHT

In a subsequent letter, "Sporting Epistle from Alabama," subtitled "Dog Story Extraordinary" and dated "East Alabama, Dec. 22, 1853," Hooper wrote that he had been sick and his doctor had given him quinine. The most important information, however, was that "A few weeks since, your correspondent was a candidate before the Legislature, for the office of Solicitor, in which race it is a matter of record, that he got a 'demnition' threshing."

Hooper went on to tell his story, of a zealous party loyalist named Mac ("who thought himself politically ruined because he missed a big fellow, three consecutive shots, with a first rate revolver"), who promoted a candidate before the legislature by promising legislators a puppy from the imminent litter of the candidate's pointer. All went well, until the voters began to compare notes and realized that a total of thirty-seven pups had been promised.

It is not surprising that Hooper would want to put some emotional distance between himself and the political process in Alabama, considering his recent "threshing," and he closed on a similar note: "Since I have lost the number of my mess (Circuit,) and can no longer write myself of the *'Ninth,'* perhaps

I shall the oftener have occasion to subscribe myself / Yours
truly / NUMBER EIGHT" (*Spirit* 23 [January 7, 1854]:553).

He had been defeated for reelection to the post of solicitor
for the Ninth District by Talladega lawyer John Jefferson Woodward, a former member of the Alabama house of representatives
and editor of the *Democratic Watchtower.* That fall had also seen
the death of his father, Archibald Maclaine Hooper, at the home
of Johnson's brother George in Crawford, Georgia.

Shortly after the election, he returned to Lafayette, where
he again edited the *Chambers Tribune.* He addressed his tasks
vigorously, soliciting new subscribers and writing humorous
sketches such as "The Speatch of Mr. Twyster, of Bunkum,
Alabama, on Stait Ade." Porter reprinted it in the *Spirit* for
March 18, 1854.

It is a shame that Simon Suggs never served in the state legislature, but if he had, his oratory would doubtless have been similar
to that of the worthy Mr. Twyster:

Mister Speaker, the free sufferins of the voters of Bunkum at the
ballad box have giv me the onner of a seet on this flore, and i rise
to let it be knone that *my* sufferins in this house will likewise all be
for Bunkum. Sur other gentle*men* may talk about patritism and progris
but i go in for Bunkum and bein elected. Wat's the good its goin
to do a feller if he givs ever sich a good vote for the Stait, ef he's
to be beet into doll rags the august follerin. Sur as I said in the beginnin
of my speatch, the free sufferins of Bunkum put me here, and ef I
can find out how my county, or a majority of it wants me to go, ile
go that way ontwell my heels flies up.

Mr. Twyster has a thing or two to say about the tax collectors,
who steal from the people. He has nothing against them personally: the three local tax collectors are his "onnuble" friends
and constituents. His view of human nature is Suggsian: "If I
know enny thing, mistur Speeker, about the human famaly,
the fust thing that natur says is to git all you kin and keep all
you git."

The main object of the Representative from Bunkum's wrath
is state aid for railroads, and not only because "rale rods" give
more men access to the taxpayers' pockets.

You see i'm agin the rale rods theyselves. sur, wat good do a rale
rod do enny boddy but town folks? sur, don't it skeer all the gaim

outen the kuntry? sur, don't it fetch all sorts of furrin diseases into the kuntry sur, the forkydeer complaint and all these uther sickness is fetch inter the kuntry on these rale rods!

Mr. Twyster goes on to tell of a man who sold his land after a train killed one of his cows. The buyer intended to build an iron-works. The seller—and Mr. Twyster—laughed at the fool, "for Jim had lived on the plais four year and never seed a bit of iron on it—only piles of crumbly brown rock" (24:521).

This heavy-handed satire places Hooper squarely on the side of the merchant-planter aristocracy as opposed to the rural, non-slave-holding class. Although Twyster makes some telling observations on human nature as it relates to the authority to levy taxes, overall he is more foolish than wise. The blatant misspelling was a device that would be employed by Artemus Ward and other "Literary Humorists" after the Civil War. One can only wonder how much Hooper's recent defeat colored his attitude toward the legislature as he wrote this disparaging burlesque speech.

Shortly after the publication of Mr. Twyster's "Speatch," Hooper's career took yet another turn: in the spring of 1854 he founded, as principal editor and part owner, the *Montgomery Mail*. Porter and other editors wished him well, and soon he moved to Montgomery, leaving his wife and two sons in Lafayette but planning to send for them in the summer. In spite of the election setback (once a judge, always a judge—unless one happens to be known as "Simon Suggs"), he was moving forward. Although he was only thirty-nine, Johnson J. Hooper was respected as an editor, a nationally acclaimed humorist, and a lawyer.

Chapter Five

Hooper of the *Mail*

Although no copy of the first issue of the *Montgomery Weekly Mail* survives, it apparently appeared on the twelfth, or more likely the thirteenth, of April 1854. Hooper was only part owner—his friend and former partner in the *Chambers Tribune,* Joseph A. Holifield, held the controlling interest in "Joseph A. Holifield & Co.," and Hooper, along with P. A. Knight, the printer, made up the "& Co."[1] Questions of financial control notwithstanding, the *Mail* was from the outset known as Hooper's paper. His editorial principles, which he declared on December 6, denied that patrons should be appeased, or that their "business, political sentiments, and social and religious views" should be considered.

Once for all, however, and for *general,* not *special* application, we desire to state, that we endeavor to do justice to all men, to avoid injuring any man in his business or reputation, and that we never seek to accomplish any object by indirection. These are our aims, kept constantly in view, and never intentionally violated. At the same time, it is proper we should add, that, in our poor way, we endeavor to give such general and local intelligence as we think will interest our readers, and never suppress this thing or that thing, because its publicity may be disagreeable to some one, if the fact be, in itself, proper for publication.[2]

For Want of a Horse

Politically, Johnson J. Hooper was accused of changing horses in mid-stream. That he did so was not really his fault, though, because his first two horses, the Whig and the American or Know-Nothing parties, foundered and died under him. A third steed, the Southern Rights Opposition party, lasted but a few short months in 1860.

Hooper's earliest allegiance was to the Whig party, with which he had been identified since he came to Alabama in 1835. He had proudly proclaimed his first paper, the *East Alabamian,* a Whig paper. In 1840, the Whigs won the presidency with William Henry Harrison. When Harrison died a month after his inauguration, John Tyler, Virginia aristocrat and former Democrat, became president. Tyler, however, had little sympathy for the American System, which Whig leader Henry Clay of Kentucky favored for internal improvements such as roads and canals. Four years of squabbling and presidential vetoes left the Whig party in disarray. Their narrow victory in 1848, when Louisiana slaveholder and military hero Zachary Taylor defeated Democrat Lewis Cass of Michigan, was to be their high water mark.

In spite of his southern background, Taylor valued the well-being of the nation as a whole over sectional partisanship and proposed a compromise he hoped would end the conflict over allowing slavery in the territories and, especially, in the new states. After bitter debate, the Compromise of 1850 was enacted. Taylor died in 1850, before the passage of the Compromise, and Millard Fillmore succeeded him and helped gain passage of the bill.

Partisans on both sides of the slavery issue were outraged, and the seeds were sown for the Whig defeat of 1852. Although the Whig candidate, General Winfield Scott, was a Virginian, he was a friend of abolitionist leader William Seward and did not endorse the Compromise. (Hooper, in turn, did not endorse Scott in the *Chambers Tribune.*) Democrat Franklin Pierce defeated Scott by a modest margin in the popular vote but crushed him in the Electoral College by 254 to 42. Hooper's 1851 pronouncement in the *Alabama Journal* of the Whig party as "dead—as dead as a mackerel"[3] gradually became a reality to be formalized in the election of 1856.

The Kansas-Nebraska Act

Thanks to the ever-increasing pressure for Westward expansion and the rapidly hardening positions of the pro- and antislavery forces, Congress found the Compromise of 1850 to be only a stopgap measure. By January 1854, Senator Stephen A. Doug-

las had prepared a bill to organize the Platte country, the area
west of Iowa and Missouri. In keeping with the Compromise
of 1850, the bill would establish that the popularly elected territorial legislatures would decide the legality of slavery for themselves.

Instead of ending or even quieting the slavery controversy
as Douglas had hoped, however, the proposed bill inflamed
sectional animosity even further. Believing that the climate of
the territories in question would preclude the sort of large-scale
agriculture that made slavery economically advantageous in the
cotton states, he compromised to appease southerners. Antislavery northerners, however, protested that by leaving the slavery
question unresolved, the bill left the door open for violation
of the Missouri Compromise of 1820, which had admitted Missouri as a slave state but had outlawed slavery north of a line,
36° 30' north latitude, running along Missouri's southern border. Bowing to southern pressure, Douglas agreed to an amend-
ment nullifying the Missouri Compromise. With the help of
the Pierce administration, the measure passed both houses of
Congress, after spirited debate.

The Kansas-Nebraska Act of 1854, rather than cooling off
the slavery dispute as intended, merely heated it up. Douglas
himself admitted that he could have traveled from Chicago to
Boston by the light of his burning effigies. The competition
to control the elections to set up the new territorial governments
would give the area the name "Bleeding Kansas" and create
the atmosphere that spawned John Brown. Elections would be
marked by bloodshed and fraud. The antislavery minister Henry
Ward Beecher once said that a rifle might be a more effective
moral agent in Kansas than a Bible, and New Englanders sent
crates of "Beecher's Bibles" to their abolitionist allies. Slavery
sympathizers known as "border ruffians" crossed the border
from Missouri into Kansas, attacking and burning free-soil settlements. (The support these raiders enjoyed in the South is sug-
gested by the name of a race horse, "Border Ruffian," which
is mentioned in some of Hooper's reports on southern horse-
races in the late 1850s.)

While the Kansas-Nebraska Act turned some northern Democrats against Douglas and failed to ingratiate him with the South,
which would always distrust him, it did even more damage to

the Whig party. Already reeling from the Compromise of 1850, the party lost many of its northern members, the "Conscience Whigs," who joined with radical abolitionists and free-soilers and a few northern Democrats to form "anti-Nebraska" groups, which would constitute the nucleus of the Republican party.[4]

Some Incidental Journalism

Thus, the Whig party in shambles, Johnson proclaimed in mid-April 1854 his new-born *Montgomery Weekly Mail* to be "Independent." Old political labels were not peeled off so easily, however, and such longtime rivals as John C. Bates of the *Journal* and P. H. Brittan of the *Advertiser* were not likely to let anyone forget Hooper's two decades and more as a Whig.

Hooper and the *Weekly Mail* progressed nicely, in spite of the intense competition for subscribers in a county with only 10,169 white citizens, along with 115 "free colored" and 19,427 slaves.[5] (This preponderance of slaves was typical of the plantation areas of the "Black Belt.") On June 10, Holifield & Co. expanded their operation by publishing the *Tri-Weekly Mail* on Tuesdays, Thursdays, and Saturdays.

Much of the success of the *Mail*s can be attributed to Hooper's editorial skill and lively writing style. During this period he wrote several humorous pieces for his own papers, and Porter, probably grateful that Hooper had broken his long silence, reprinted them in volume 24 of the *Spirit of the Times.* Although some of the anecdotes might entice a smile from a reader, their abbreviated length and diluted quality show that Hooper no longer had the time, energy, or interest to produce work of the quality and scope of the Suggs tales or even *A Ride with Old Kit Kuncker.*

Another of his sketches, "Sloshin' About," was copied by *Harper's New Monthly Magazine* in October 1854, with the following notice: "The Montgomery (Alabama) *Mail,* seems to have a fund of humor on hand, and gives occasionally a South-western sketch by a few touches, that are as telling as Hogarth's."

In Pike County, there was a trial for a "general row," and a witness testified that one Saltonstall, *"jest kept sloshin' about."* This remark was frequently repeated, and the lawyer for the defense asked the witness to explain Saltonstall's connection with the affair. "Saltonstall? Why, I've told you several times; the rest on 'em clinched and paired off, but *Saltonstall, he jest kept sloshin' about."* The witness explained that the other participants in the affray "was all together on the ground, a-bitin', gougin', and kickin' one another," all "legle" forms of social intercourse in Pike County, but the "chivalrous" Saltonstall "made it his business to walk backward and forward through the crowd, with a big stick in his hand, and knock down every loose man in the crowd as fast as he come to 'em! That's what I call SLOSHIN' ABOUT!" (9:701).

Just two months later, in December, *Harper's* would lose the handle to a Hooper story, as it reprinted "A Georgia Major" explaining that they thought the author might be "an acquaintance of . . . Judge Longstreeet."

Hooper thought *Harper's* had attributed the piece to A. B. Longstreet, and he commented in the *Daily Mail* for December 2: "The last *Harper* [*sic*] publishes a little sketch written by us, years ago, entitled *The Georgia Major,* and credits it to Judge Longstreet. Of all the undeserved compliments we ever received, this is the highest" (2, col. 1). The "little sketch" is vivid and amusing, and perhaps "years ago" is the key phrase, for it is first-rate Hooper.

The Georgia Major is on trial before the Mayor for assault and battery on the person of the Rev. Mr. Williams. He pleads guilty on the first count. When the Mayor learns that the minister's offense was to address the Major without removing his hat, he fines the Major ten dollars and costs. The second charge stems from a subsequent fight between the Major and the minister. The Major insists that the crowd jumped on him and beat him. A witness, however, testifies that no one other than the minister laid a hand on the Major. The Major is quite surprised by this revelation, that his imagination had magnified one man of not over 150 pounds into a crowd.

The Mayor rules that the Major has been punished enough by the fine and the whipping, and the Major is mortified. He would rather be fined $500 than have it entered on the record that he was whipped and begins to strut about the room proclaiming he has never been whipped. When someone in the crowd remarks that that could be arranged, "the Major collapsed into his original dimensions, in the folding of a peacock's tail;

and wiping the perspiration from his brow, quietly retired."
This little masterpiece of characterization serves as a reminder
of what Hooper was capable of when he turned his mind away
from politics.

More *Mails*

According to W. Stanley Hoole, Hooper's family was able
to join him in Montgomery by late summer.[6] Marion Kelley,
however, reports that Hooper moved in early 1855 to the Exchange Hotel, and that Mrs. Hooper "had not yet moved to
Montgomery."[7] Baptismal records unearthed by Hoole show
that William DeBerniere and Adolphus Stanford Hooper were
baptized in St. John's Episcopal Church, Montgomery, on November 30, 1854, by Bishop Nicholas H. Cobbs.[8] Even this
is not conclusive evidence that the family had actually taken
up residence in Montgomery.

About this time, perhaps during October (gaps in the surviving issues of the various *Montgomery Mails* make exact dating
difficult), Hooper fell victim to the yellow-fever epidemic that
had swept Montgomery. His case was apparently not serious,
for the *Cassville* [Georgia] *Standard* wrote:

We are rejoiced to know that our beau ideal of a first rate editor,
Jonce Hooper, is at his post again. The yellow fever may have frightened
him pretty badly, but it hasn't *scared* all the fun out of him, by a jug
full, for the last number of his paper is running over with good things.[9]

As if a *Weekly Mail* and a *Tri-Weekly Mail* were not enough,
Holifield & Co. began on November 16 to publish the *Montgomery Daily Mail.* Like other papers of the day, it presented an
appearance quite different from today's newspapers. The front
page was occupied primarily by ads, such as "The Blind See,"
which acquainted the *Mail*'s readers with Ball's Eye Cups, sold
by "Sam. Swan, General Agent, Sign of the Bronze Lion." For
some time during the *Daily Mail*'s infancy, Hooper reprinted
the "Free School Law" of 1851 on page one, and during Fair
Week, late October and early November, he ran and reran
an editorial, "BEWARE OF PICKPOCKETS," under "Local Intelligence." Throughout the paper's four pages were scattered other

ads, among them "Sir Astley Cooper Bart, M.D.'s 'Medicated Fur Chest Protector,' " hailed as a "Great Preventative of Consumption and Unfailing Cure for Pulmonary Diseases." On page three Hooper generally ran the tuition rates of the Presbyterian Collegiate Female Institute at Talladega, Alabama, including: "Preparatory Dept. $10, Collegiate Dept. $20, Languages $5, Piano $20, Drawing $10," and "Paper Flowers $5."

On pages two and three appeared the news, with accounts often copied from papers all over the country: the latest steamship arrival, the most recent train and steamboat accidents, and telegraph reports of foreign events. Under "Local Matters" and "Local Intelligence" Hooper printed anecdotes, remarks about the weather, accounts of fist fights, a notice of such rarities as a 124-pound squash on display at Coxe and Hutchings's drug store,[10] and, on Mondays, summaries of sermons at St. John's Episcopal, the Methodist Episcopal, and the Baptist Church. On September 15, 1855, he announced in *"A Very Sad Misfortune"*: "A grievous ill befell our city yesterday. Every citizen bewails it, with a sincerity which cannot be doubted. *Our Ice gave out!"* (3, col. 1). On October 8, 1855, he rejoiced in the frost, which he hoped would end the malaria epidemic (3, col. 1).

On page three he periodically published the burial list for the month. On November 3, 1855, for example, he posted the city sexton's report for October. "Whites" are listed by name, and "Blacks" by owner as follows: "A negro child of Gen. Carroll" (3, col. 1). Typical editorials attacked "High Prices in Montgomery" (November 23, 1854, 2, col. 1) and "Public Executions" (January 6, 1855, 3, col. 1).

Like the other two *Mail*s, the *Daily Mail* was an "Independent Paper," and Hooper was primarily responsible for its contents. The new paper's reception by the southern press indicates the high esteem in which Hooper was held by his fellow editors. The *Cassville* [Ga.] *Standard* noted: . . . "we see that the *Mail* is now published *daily* as well as weekly. Well, we don't wonder at it, for we can't very well see how *Jonce's* subscribers could do without a *daily mail*, when he has the job of MAKING IT UP." The *Macon* [Georgia] *Republican* pronounced it a "beautiful sheet."[11]

Hooper's filler included some humorous sketches, such as

"Tail Told" (November 21, 1854, 3 col. 1), "The Town Cow" (November 22, 3 col. 1), "Valor and Prudence—but Mostly Prudence" (November 24, 3 col. 1), and "Matched to a Hair" (November 18, 1854, 3 col. 1). Only one of these unexceptional anecdotes was chosen by Porter for the *Spirit,* and that was the horse-swap tale, "Matched to a Hair," which appeared on December 16, 1854 (24:521).

Strange Bedfellows:
Hooper and the Know-Nothings

With the southern Whigs and the northern "Conscience Whigs" unable to reconcile their differences, southern members like Hooper were faced with a dilemma: should they remain loyal to a party with a strong abolitionist element or align themselves with their longtime foe, the Democratic party of Andrew Jackson? Unable to stomach either choice, by 1854 many southern Whigs were turning to the new American or "Know-Nothing" party.

In the 1840s and 1850s northern Protestants, alarmed by the mounting tide of German Catholic and, especially, Irish Catholic immigrants, had begun to form secret societies with names like the Druids and the Sons of America. They were sworn to secrecy about their goals and activities, and thus came to be called "Know-Nothings." They began to translate their aims of maintaining Protestant supremacy and curtailing immigration into political action and profited greatly from the break-up of the Whig party after Scott's defeat in 1852. Hooper was one of those southern Whigs who turned in desperation to the American party.

In Alabama, the Know-Nothings first showed their strength in the election of 1855. Union Democrat John A. Winston, the controversial "Veto Governor," was running for reelection against State Aid Democrat Robert A. Baker and American party candidate George D. Shortridge. Dropping the *Mail*'s "Independent" label, Hooper began the year endorsing Baker for governor and Thomas H. Watts for Congress.

In that same month of January, Hooper went to Mobile to

report on the Know-Nothings' state convention. While there
he stayed at the renowned Battle House Hotel, which he wrote
about glowingly in his dispatches back to the *Mail.* His journalistic integrity, however, compelled him to observe that the fruit
was *"inferior"* and the music of the Master of Gongs altogether
too loud. That Johnson J. Hooper had come a long way from
the Lafayette lawyer and the Wetumpka editor is shown by
accounts of his meetings with thespians Dion Boucicault and
Agnes Robertson; General Mirabeau B. Lamar, who had once
been President of Texas; and Clark Mills, sculptor of a famous—
if controversial—statue of Andrew Jackson. Mills showed
Hooper a metal miniature of the statue, which Hooper defended
against "the newspaper criticisms which sought to induce the
belief that the equestrian statue is a humbug."[12] Apart from
the enclosure of Hero in quotation marks, there is no trace of
the anti-Jacksonian irreverence that had led Hooper the Whig
to mock Old Hickory in "Taking the Census" and *Adventures
of Simon Suggs* a few years earlier.

By June 7, Hooper was lauding the American party's George
D. Shortridge, although he and the *Daily Mail* still nominally
backed Baker. Shortridge himself, however, was in favor of
state aid for railroads and other internal improvements, a major
consideration for former Whigs like Hooper. (Recall Henry
Clay's American Plan and Hooper's satire on "Mr. Twyster
from Bunkum," the nearly illiterate bumpkin who was against
"Stait Aid.") The day the Know-Nothings convened in Montgomery later that month, Hooper commended Shortridge editorially for his stands on State Aid and Temperance. (While
Hooper was hardly a Temperance advocate, as his social habits
and some of his humor show, he recognized their political clout.)
On June 14, he printed the "American" platform in the *Daily
Mail* (2, col. 2), dropping at last the name of Robert A. Baker.
On June 22, he announced: "We run up the name of Judge
Shortridge, to-day," although his endorsement fell short of enthusiastic: "because we think that *on the whole* he is a little more
liberal in his views in regard to State aied [*sic*], than his opponent. If we cannot get a whole loaf, we will e'en try to get a
half one!" (2, col. 1).

Presently a Know-Nothing and longtime Union supporter,
Hooper nevertheless made it plain that "Southern Patriotism"

was most important to him. As early as November 20, 1854, he had written:

Zealous unionists as we have always been, . . . when the question is upon the preservation, *beyond the probability of danger,* of the institution of slavery, we should not hesitate to vote for a dissolution of any connection which brought that institution into the *slightest* jeopardy. In other words, we would not imperil slavery for a thousand Unions. . . .[13]

According to Hoole, "Thus did the *Mail* slowly become the state's most prominent newspaper for the Southern Rights wing of the 'Know Nothing' party and as such was a powerful anti-Democratic influence from 1855 to the Civil War."[14]

The campaign of 1855 was a bitter and spirited one, high-lighted—or lowlighted—by editorial duels such as those be-tween Hooper's American *Mail* and P. H. Brittan's *Montgomery Advertiser,* which, on April 5, 1855, characterized the American party as "bound together by the selfishness that marks envious imbecility, and grows by the aggregate of the small things that crawl and buzz over the body of dead Whiggery."[15]

Hooper, for his part, enthusiastically attacked the "Bogus Democrats" and matched the *Advertiser* epithet for epithet. On July 17 he remarked concerning a law to prohibit illiterates from serving on juries: "We think the law was a wise one; . . . But the *Advertiser* pretends to think differently, and yet sustained one of its supporters, for a high judicial office. There's the quintessence of duplicity for you!" (2, col. 1).

Three days later, his temperature having risen considerably, he deplored the "vile, calumnious attack on Judge Rice" made by the **"Raving, Maddened Advertiser,"** observing metaphori-cally: "The blinded rattle-snake continues to strike its fangs into its own body, and the public watch the developments of the poisons" (July 20, 2, col 1).

There were preelection riots in Mobile, but the balloting itself was conducted without violence. When the dust had settled, the Democrat Winston had beaten the Know-Nothing Shortridge by 42,000 to 30,000, although the American party had polled the largest vote ever against a Democratic candidate for governor. For Hooper, there was the added solace of knowing that his own Montgomery County and adjoining Macon and Lowndes were among the fifteen carried by the new party. His candidate for Congress, Watts, had also lost, though narrowly, to Democrat James F. Dowdell.[16]

To the delight of his foes, he presented the results as a moral victory, rather than a defeat, and reaffirmed his party's commitment to the South:

This new party has not carried Alabama, on its first trial; but it has *made its mark*. Its foundation is *"the constitutson* [*sic*] *of the United States; the rights of the States; Protestantism and a free Bible; and the rule of Americans over their own country."*

These principles must, ere long, command the approval of the people of Alabama, and of the entire South.[17]

A Hard Road

In addition to the heavy demands of the election campaign, Hooper also during that time had difficulties with his own health and with the financial health of the *Mail.* For a few days in July he was forced to stay in his room at the Exchange Hotel, and in August he returned home to Lafayette and his family at the advice of his physician for "some days, perhaps weeks, in the quiet of the country."[18] Upon his return he thanked editorially friends who had helped out in his absence.

The relief was only temporary, however, as Montgomery's yellow-fever outbreak reached epidemic proportions. On September 26, 1855, he wrote in the *Daily Mail:*

"**A Hard Road!**"—We find many obstacles already, in consequence of the panic, in the way of getting out the *Mail.* We are minus two hands this morning, and a third will leave to-night. Our subscribers must bear with us. . . . If, however, we can keep a hand or two, we shall issue some sort of a sheet, every day. (2, col. 1)

The road grew harder, though, as Hooper himself succumbed to yellow fever barely a week later. Friends rallied to him, and upon his return on October 8, he expressed his gratitude for their "kindness . . . which kept the *Mail* going, and its editor well doctored, nursed, and tended, during a very dull, unpleasant time." He especially expressed "our gratification at the evidences of sympathy from our old and valued friend, [John C.] BATES, of the [Alabama] *Journal.* There are some natures which do not change or grow cold by any lapse of time or alteration of circumstances; and the Major's is one of them" (2, col. 1).

Even in times of crisis, the give and take of friendly editorial humor continued. Three days later Hooper wrote in the *Daily Mail* for October 11: "Think of a convalescent receiving such a letter as this:

_____ Ala., Oct. 6, 1855

Dear H____:

Hear you are dead of yellow fever. Have bet $10 to $5 *against it,* going on the general principle that you would get up some irrelevant and immaterial issue with 'D____ and the D____'; and beat 'em on it. Send me a line under your own hand, that I may draw stakes.

Yours confidently,
C____" (2, col. 1)

Compounding the ravages of yellow fever, the various *Mail*s were in financial difficulty during this period. On January 25, 1855, a maxim in the columns of the *Daily Mail* quipped: "If exercise promotes health, those who collect old bills for editors should be among the longest lived people on earth (2, col. 2). On September 24, he pleaded for "such of our patrons as approve the [American party] sentiments of this paper . . ." to help increase the *Mail*'s subscriber list (2, col. 1).

By October 10 Hooper's tone had grown more desperate:

INDISPENSABLY NECESSARY—It is absolutely essential to us, that our negligent subscribers should immediately remit us their subscriptions. . . . There is no use mincing matters; we cannot publish, if we cannot get money. . . . We have been fighting for eighteen months, against an unbroken series of adverse circumstances; and now, with greatly enfeebled health, our sole reliance is on the punctuality of our patrons. . . . our weekly circulation is the second in town, and ought alone to suffice nearly to pay our expenses. And yet we are pressed beyond endurance! (2, col. 1)

Survive the *Mail* did, however, and, according to Hoole, "Hooper personally continued to grow in the esteem of his fellow-citizens, both his political friends and enemies."[19] In September he was elected secretary of the "Aid to Virginia Cities" committee, Thomas H. Watts Chairman, for yellow-fever relief.[20] Also (keep in mind that dogs were not something a gentleman took lightly), he was picked for the Montgomery State Fair's "Committee on Terrier Dogs." Hooper himself commented in the *Daily Mail* for November 2: "Of ourself, it would be immodest to speak, further than to say, we are the friend of the race . . ." (2, col. 2). Thus, in spite of political, physical, and financial adversity—or rather because of his courage and grace in facing up to them—Johnson J. Hooper was gaining the respect of people in the Montgomery community and beyond.

Politics as Usual

When the Democrat-dominated legislature met on November 12, 1855, Hooper was there to cover the Democratic caucus, both as a reporter for the *Mail* and as a private pamphleteer. The fruit of this latter effort was a sixteen-page pamphlet: *Read and Circulate: Proceedings of the Democratic and Anti-Know-Nothing Party, in Caucus; or the Guillotine at Work, at the Capital, During the Session of 1855–'56,* by "An Eye Witness." Hooper reported the events of the caucus straightforwardly, for the most part, although traces of irony may be detected:

At 7½ o'clock, the Hon. Mr. Smith, of Lauderdale, took the Chair, and with his usual dignity and self-complacency, called the Caucus to order. . . .

Some gentleman called for Gov. Chapman, when that gentleman stepped forward and exclaimed, *"I am here!"* whereat the Caucus applauded most enthusiastically, as though it was thought some point was gained.[21]

As indicated by the inscription, "To the Memory of the Unfortunate Victims of the Sanguinary Guillotine Is This Report of Its Workings Most Feelingly and Respectfully Dedicated by the Reporter," Hooper was critical of the caucus system and the uncompromising way in which the Democrats were excluding any members suspected of the Know-Nothing heresy. He took pains to point out that most of the nominating speeches included a statement that the nominee was—or "has always been"—"a good Democrat and an anti–Know Nothing."

Coincidentally, Hooper's old friend and the original of Simon Suggs, Bird Young, was nominated for adjutant general. He led after the first ballot, but his strength faded (there had been an accusation that Young "has seen the elephant," that he had Know-Nothing leanings), and another was chosen as the party's nominee. Hooper himself received a vote on the second and third ballots. Although he added a waggish footnote: ("* Hooper of course was no candidate—he does not belong to the King" [9]), he passed up this obvious chance to resurrect the memory of Simon Suggs. In truth, the day was past when he would call attention to the waggery of his youth. (Some months later, in March 1857, Hooper reprinted in the *Mail* a column from the *Camden* [Alabama] *Republic* backing Bird Young for governor of Alabama. Although the *Republic* invoked memories of Simon Suggs, Hooper commented only that he thought Young would make "an admirable representative in the gubernatorial field of anti–State Aid Democracy.")[22]

While the caucus was still in session, on November 20, 1855, Hooper published in the *Daily Mail* a poem that summed up his attitude toward the caucus system:

> Old King Caw is a jolly old cuss,
> And he gets his friends out of many a muss;
> He hasn't got a "lodge" but a sly old Hole,
> And it's there the old King calls his roll!
> King Caw! King Caw!
> Caw! Caw! Caw! Caw!
> It's a jolly old cock that makes the law.[23]

With commendable good sportsmanship, considering the bitterness of the campaign just concluded, he added some months later: "We have met the enemy, and—we are theirs!" So exceptional was this gesture that he was quoted in the *Wetumpka Whig,* the *St. Louis Reveille, Freeman's Journal,* and the *Spirit of the Times.*[24]

Still a Know-Nothing

In 1856 Hooper consolidated his journalistic gains: after some shifts in ownership, he emerged as the "Senior Editor" and the senior partner in "Hooper and Coyne," which controlled all three *Mails*. His notes for $2,300 were secured by his American-party allies Thomas H. Watts and Thomas J. Judge, the former having narrowly lost in the recent congressional election.[25] With his new junior partner, Henry E. Coyne, who had been a foreman on the competing *Alabama Journal,* Hooper worked well and amicably. In the *Mail*'s new offices, on the old courthouse "Square," which was not a square at all,[26] Hooper was at last established as an editor.

Political security was another matter. While he was certain of his principles—for the Union but more strongly for "Southern Patriotism" and against Abolitionism—finding an adequate vehicle for them was something else. The brave showing, the moral victory in the state-level elections of 1855, rather than being the dawning of a new day for the American or Know-Nothing party, was actually high noon.

Much of the appeal of the Know-Nothings in the North was based on anti-Catholic and antiimmigrant bigotry: in 1855, Know-Nothings captured every state office and most of the seats in the state legislature of Massachusetts, that hotbed of antislavery sentiment. While southerners approved of the American-party plank opposing voting rights for unnaturalized foreigners in the territories and mistrusted the influx of immigrants that was swelling the population of the northern states and manning, womaning, and childing its factories with cheap labor, they, like so many others, were uneasy with the Know-Nothings' violent hostility to America's traditional respect for freedom of religion. Hooper was one of these southern Know-Nothings who put up with the party's intolerance primarily because there seemed no better political hope for the South. He opposed the Americans' religious intolerance editorially: "We have regarded it, *if true* as a very strong point of objection."[27]

Other editorials, however, show that the editor of the *Mail* was not as tolerant as some scholars have represented him. "Fights Among the Jews," in the *Daily Mail* for November 3, 1856 (3, col. 1), noted that "The chosen people have been indulging their pugnacious proclivities within the last week. They generally come out second best." Fighting in this context did not seem to entertain Hooper as it had in so many instances in the past, instances that inspired such high-spirited tales as "Jim Bell's Revenge."

On another occasion he echoed the American party line in

"Matters for Reflection" (*Daily Mail,* July 26, 1855, 2, col. 1):

The surest mode of keeping this country republican, is to keep it Protestant. . . .
Why are the bogus-democrats working so hard for the foreigners as well as for the Catholics? Do the people wish *to increase the power of foreigners and Catholics in this country?* If so, they ought to oppose the American party, and act with the bogus-democrats.

Of particular concern to Hooper were the German settlements in Texas, one of which flew the German flag and another of which published a German-language abolitionist paper, *Die Zietung.* In addition to denouncing such communities, in "Germans in Texas" (*Daily Mail,* August 25, 1855, 2, col. 2), he reprinted "The Perils of Lager Bier," from the *Scalpel* (November 11, 1856, 2, col. 2).

In late 1855 the Alabama Know-Nothings had voted to abolish all party restrictions on religious freedom,[28] contradicting the national party's platform. Nevertheless, in February 1856 the Alabama party's state council, of which Hooper, along with Watts and others, was a leader, formulated its principles and chose its delegates to the national convention to be held in Philadelphia. Once at the convention, however, the Alabama delegation found that not only was the national party's position on religion too intolerant, but it did not go far enough in support of the South's commitment to slavery. The Know-Nothings nominated Millard Fillmore of New York, a former Whig who, it will be recalled, had served out Zachary Taylor's unfinished presidential term from 1850 to 1853.

The Democrats, whose lack of accomplishment during the administration of Franklin Pierce provided scant recommendation to the voters, nominated James Buchanan of Pennsylvania, whom mid-twentieth-century historians characterize as "a Northern man with Southern principles . . . elderly and undistinguished, less principled than partisan." [29]

Hooper, however, commended Buchanan editorially as "the only statesman before the Convention . . . , a statesman who has given eminent services to the country. . . ."[30] (As Kelley writes, Hooper "was always tolerant and far-sighted enough to keep personalities out of his editorials and to attack the princi-

ples of a man.'') [31] Johnson's judgment was a comparative one,
made in the light of Buchanan's opponents, ineffectual incumbent Franklin Pierce and Illinois's Stephen A. Douglas, whose
efforts to save the Union by compromise had earned him the
scorn and even hatred of proslavery and abolitionist forces alike,
to whom Buchanan was ''vastly superior'' ''in all moral, intellectual and political points.''[32]

The Rise of the "Black Republicans"

If the American party had sprouted and bloomed in a day,
and would wither before nightfall, another new political party
was to flourish and grow into a leafy giant that would cast its
shade over the South for decades to come.

As mentioned previously, the Kansas-Nebraska Act of 1854
had jarred the Democratic party and, especially, the Whig party,
sending northern, antislavery factions spinning off. The scattered
elements began to coalesce around nuclei of ''anti-Nebraska''
groups. One of these, in Ripon, Wisconsin, devoted itself to
forming a new party, whose principal platform would be resis-
tance to the expansion of slavery. This new party rapidly took
shape and adopted the name ''Republican.'' To its banner
flocked not only antislavery Democrats, Whigs, and free-soilers
but also temperance advocates, nativists who found the Know-
Nothings too much for them, and the inevitable political oppor-
tunists.

From these beginnings in 1854, the numbers and strength
of the Republicans grew astonishingly, as demonstrated by their
successes in northern state elections in 1855. Having gained
control of most of the northern state governments, they adopted
a strong free-soil platform sure to alienate southern voters. However, while maintaining that Congress should prohibit slavery
in the territories, they did not go so far as to demand or even
recommend abolition of slavery in states that already had it.
They nominated John C. Fremont, western explorer and soldier,
an antislavery man.[33]

The Election of 1856

Although many of the Alabama Know-Nothings rejected Millard Fillmore, Hooper maintained nominal support and kept

the party ticket of Fillmore and Andrew J. Donelson on the masthead of the *Mail.*

National events had passions boiling on both sides of the Mason-Dixon Line, and in May a band of Missouri "border ruffians" sacked the free-soil town of Lawrence, Kansas. Abolitionist John Brown and his sons retaliated by killing five proslavery settlers. There was yet another proslavery counterattack before federal troops intervened.

On May 19, abolitionist senator Charles Sumner of Massachusetts delivered an impassioned speech, "The Crime against Kansas." He made vicious personal attacks on South Carolina senator Andrew Pickens Butler, who was absent from the chamber at the time. Butler's nephew, Congressman Preston Brooks, also of South Carolina, defended his uncle's honor on the floor of the Senate two days later by severely beating Sumner with a cane. Sumner never fully recovered from the injuries, and it was several years before he could return to the Senate. (Just a year and a half earlier, *Harper's New Monthly Magazine,* published in New York, had found amusing Hooper's account of the gentleman who *"jest kept sloshin' about"* with a big stick, knocking down "every loose man in the crowd as fast as he come to 'em.") While Sumner became a martyr to the antislavery North, Brooks was a hero to his fellow southerners. Hooper of the *Mail* was one of those who applauded his exploits with the quarterstaff. When Brooks died in 1857, Hooper printed "Lines in Memory of Preston S. Brooks," by John W. Stokes:

> To Brooks, whose kind, whose brave and loving heart,
> Fulfilled a statesman's, hero's and a patriot's part;
> . . . .
> *Bold* in reproof, yet gentle in command,
> He spread "fraternal zeal" throughout the land,
> And led all arms to act, all hearts to feel,
> What Southern valor owed to Southern weal . . .[34]

The growing foreboding with which southerners had come to regard national politics may be seen in Hooper's editorial explanation of his decision to give all his employees the day off on July 4: "Perhaps this is the last Fourth of July the American people will ever celebrate *as one nation.* Let us all, therefore, 'take a chance at it.' "[35]

Although there were three candidates, the race in the South was between the Democrat Buchanan and the American Fillmore. In Alabama, Democrat William Lowndes Yancey provided most of the oratorical fireworks. Although he easily handled any debate opponent the Know-Nothings put up against him, his chief whipping boy was "Black Republicanism," and his principal cause was Southern Rights. According to Alabama historian A. B. Moore, "Old Whig disciples came to sit as interested spectators, but left converts to the new creed of Southern Rights,"[36] Johnson J. Hooper was not a new convert to this creed, but he was undoubtedly impressed by Yancey's eloquence. Before long, the two men would make common cause.

When the furor had subsided, the American party's Fillmore had finished a distant third, with the eight electoral votes of Maryland and 21 percent of the popular vote. The victorious Democrat Buchanan had 174 electoral votes to Republican Fremont's 117, but he had polled only 45 percent of the popular vote. Without winning a single southern state, the Republicans had come so close to victory that they would have won if they had carried Pennsylvania and either Indiana or Illinois.[37]

In Alabama's two-horse race, Buchanan beat Fillmore by a two-to-one margin. The Know-Nothings carried only seven counties. As in the state elections of 1855, the three Whig counties served by the *Mail,* Montgomery, Macon, and Lowndes, went for the Know-Nothing candidate. Hooper's friend Thomas J. Judge, like him a Whig turned Know-Nothing, lost the congressional election to Democrat David Clopton by a mere 214 votes out of over 13,000 cast.[38]

In classic Know-Nothing fashion, Hooper acknowledged the outcome in the *Daily Mail* for November 5, 1856:

WE SALUTE THE POPE!

The returns of the election, so far as they have come in, look very unfavorable for the American Party. We are inclined to think that His Holiness, Pope Pius, has given us K.N.'s a confounded walloping. If it should prove so, we shall knock under to His Holiness, as good-humoredly as we can, and admit that he has taken the starch out of Young America." (2, col. 1)

In a few short years, at the close of his life, Johnson would have an altogether different attitude toward His Holiness.

Aside from this outburst, however, Hooper rose to this occasion to prove himself once more the gracious loser. Democrats' jubilation was unrestrained, as the *Wetumpka Dispatch* trumpeted: "No North, No South, No East, No Where, *Know Nothing.*"³⁹ He acknowledged in the *Daily Mail* the receipt of "a FILLMOURNER Hat," an "antique mourning bonnet, of the blackest black and the most diabolical cut. . . . These delicate little attentions of our Democratic friends have multiplied on us lately. Last week, we were made *Barber* on one Salt River Steamer and *Engineer* on another."⁴⁰ He did find ammunition for a jovial counterattack, noting that some of the celebrants had but recently crossed over to the Democrats, the *"strong side"*: "They feel it is *'we'* who are successful—who have the President—who beat the Know Nothings—and who now have the right of admission into 'good society' in Montgomery. Ah, these fellows are happy—nobody happier, barring the Dutch!"⁴¹

Return to the *Spirit*

There was a brief revival of the relationship between Hooper and his longtime editorial friend and benefactor, William T. Porter, as Porter reprinted from the *Mail* a few pieces, the authorship of which is difficult to ascribe. One, "Old Mammy Halladay's Experience," is a dialect account of an old black woman's religious experience.⁴² Porter introduced "In Favor of the Hog" on the same page: "We find the following communication in the Montgomery Mail. It has a peculiarity about it which, to us, is an evidence that Jonce Hooper himself had a hand in dressing it up."

Indeed, there is much of Hooper in the tone and substance of "In Favor of the Hog," a tale of frontier justice:

In the good old county of C____, State of Alabama, there lived one John Smith, who . . . was peculiarly afflicted with a want of discrimination between his own things and those of other persons, or who, rather, was ignorant of the laws relating to *"meum et tuum."*

Caught stealing a hog, John was bound over to a jury and found "Guilty of hog stealing in the first degree." The Judge told the jury that there is no degree to hog stealing and instructed them to bring in their verdict in proper form. Deliberating once more, they returned the verdict: *"We, the jeurey, pusilani-mously find the defendant gilty in the sum of 1 dollar and ½ in favor of the hog."*[43]

Late in the summer of 1856, Porter left the *Spirit* and began his own paper, *Porter's Spirit of the Times.* He asked for assistance. Hooper responded warmly, wishing him luck and assuring him: "I shall be with you, *sure!"* Although he was not certain just how soon he could send something, he concluded graciously: "and the 'Spirit of the Times,' 'made perfeck,' by the prefix of 'Porter's,' will become a 'harp of a thousand strings,' on which we will all want to play." In a final burst of nostalgia, he signed the letter "Simon Suggs."[44] Nothing came of his good intentions, however.

Simon Goes to Savannah and Is "Done" to a Cracklin'

No doubt grateful that the partisan strife of the election was over, Hooper threw himself in November and December into preparations for the eleventh Southern Commercial Convention, to be held in Savannah, Georgia. Ten states sent 564 delegates. Hooper was secretary of the fifty-member Alabama delegation. Well before the convention he stepped up the boosting of the South, which had been a part of his editorial policy for some time:

We have *talked* the South into a belief . . . that all the elements of progress, social, moral and commercial, abound in our people; and it remains only to cause, in some way, a practical development of the theory to such an extent as will convince not only *our own doubters, but the world.*[45]

On the eve of his departure, he joked: "A malicious person here suggests that though we may go down *Hooper,* it may be necessary to send us back *Hooped.* We expect, however, to come back as we shall go down, *under a cloud."*[46] This was truer than he knew.

Some indication of Hooper's stature may be gathered from the attention paid him by other members of the press, including such papers as the *Alabama Journal,* the *Savannah Republican,* and the *Savannah News,* the latter of which welcomed him as follows: "Among the members of the pen and scissors fraternity . . . is Johnson J. Hooper. . . .—We only mention the fact by way of correcting a gross slander against him. Like the old gentleman of whom we read, he ain't half so ugly as he's painted." [47]

Hooper's partner, Henry Coyne, "the Junior," who was back in Montgomery minding the store, got in on the fun, defending "JONCENG . . . 'The Ugly Man,' " with tongue in cheek: "when he 'slicks up' and goes abroad, he's considered as good looking as—common folks. Seriously, he IS good looking, and would be so called by competent judges anywhere—(if they didn't care what they said)." [48]

On December 8 occurred the event that has been noted by all of Hooper's biographers, because it is the sort of moment that lends itself so naturally to dramatizing and moralizing. The only problem is that its source is William Garrett, a Democrat and former Alabama secretary of state, a man whose political background and writing demonstrate his hostility to Hooper. According to Garrett, while the convention was waiting for a special committee to return to report the permanent officers,

. . . Judge John A. Jones, of Georgia, himself a wag and humorist, formally moved, in presence of the six or eight hundred delegates, that Simon Suggs be called upon to give an account of himself for the last two years. The Mayor, with great politeness, put the question, and on its being carried in the affirmative by a unanimous vote, he requested "Mr. Suggs," if present, to comply with the expressed desire of the Convention. There sat Mr. Hooper in the pit, wrapped in a green blanket coat, near Albert Pike, of Arkansas, as if overwhelmed by the pressure. . . . He stirred not an inch. More than a thousand persons, in the galleries and elsewhere, were on the tiptoe of expectation at hearing "Simon Suggs" deliver his convulsive jokes. But the feast came not, when the entrance of the committee put an end to the embarrassment of Mr. Hooper.

Later, as Garrett tells it, Judge Jones referred to the incident as evidence of Hooper's popularity. The editor of the *Mail,* however,

replied that a liberty had been taken with his name which was really offensive, as showing that others looked upon him as a mere story-

teller, with nothing solid in his composition. He confessed and regretted that his writings had established that character in public estimation,
and that he felt its depressing influence whenever he desired, or aimed,
to soar above it, to a higher rank before the public. His ambition
had been to move in quite a different channel, to enjoy the respect
of men; but he had unfortunately obtained a reputation which cut
off all such hopes. It was an evil day to his fortunes and to his happiness
when he embarked in that class of literature, or otherwise became a
chronic story-teller for the diversion of his companions. He said it
was probably too late to rectify the blunder, and that he must continue
to suffer the consequences.

Garrett continues:

For once in his life, Mr. Hooper appeared to be in earnest, while
deploring his *notoriety*. There is a salutary moral in his experience
which, it is hoped, may have the effect on others to cultivate habitual
self-respect and a due regard for public opinion, while cherishing at
all times lofty feelings and resolutions to possess the gold of character,
without the alloy which defeated the genius of Johnson J. Hooper.
Here let him stand as a beaconlight, to give warning of the rock on
which the manly ambition and hopes of his youth perished.[49]

Another contemporary account of the convention casts doubt
on at least some details of Garrett's story. The report of
H. B. D. De Bow, a delegate from Louisiana who wrote up
the convention for his *Review,* makes no mention of the incident.
In addition, he lists "Col. J. J. Hooper" (Jonce seems to have
made colonel even more easily than Simon became captain)
as a member of the joint committee to choose permanent officers
for the convention: "On the motion of Mr. Brown, of Maryland,
the Convention, at half past one o'clock, took a recess until 4
P.M. At 4 P.M. the Convention was called to order by the temporary chairman." Therefore, Hooper would not have been on
the floor for Judge Jones to demand of him "an account of
himself."[50]
Nevertheless, Garrett's story rings true: Hooper did, from
the mid-1850s on, downplay his comic talent in order to empha-
size his abilities as an editor and political writer. Also, other
contemporary sources report that Hooper expressed regret at
having written *Simon Suggs.*[51]

In his own reporting of the convention, Hooper made no mention of the "liberty" taken with his name—if indeed any ever was—concentrating instead on the many hopeful proposals for a Pacific Coast railroad, direct trade with Europe (the Yankee domination of foreign trade had long been a sore point with the South), and, that perennial favorite, the reopening of the slave trade.

Chapter Six

Alarms and Diversions

Dog and Gun

The *Mail* continued to thrive, and by late 1856 Hooper could boast of *"the* LARGEST CIRCULATION of any political paper in the interior of the state, by six or seven hundred copies—with but one exception." The *Grenada* [Mississippi] *Locomotive* called the *Weekly Mail* "the very handsomest paper in *Alabama."* [1]

Also during this period Hooper was busy with another project: *Dog and Gun; A Few Loose Chapters on Shooting,* [2] the last of his books that would contain much of his own writing. The volume is quite serious, and, to add to the gravity of his subject, he quotes such authorities as Roger Ascham, sixteenth-century English didactic writer, author of "The Scholemaster" and "Toxiphilus," a treatise on archery; and John Gay, another Englishman, the author of "Rural Sports" (1703).

A few titles from the book's thirteen chapters give an idea of its flavor: "I: The Gentleman's Amusement," "II: How to Choose a Good Gun," "IV: The Setter and Pointer," and "XII: Treatment of the Distemper." Chapter 1 is consistent with his citing of august predecessors:

My young sporting friends will observe, that in my title I fortify my own opinion of the manliness and innocence of Field Sports with a classic authority, while the quotation from the bard, shows our theme not wanting in poetic dignity. . . . but while the advocate of Dog and Gun is backed by old *Ascham,* and a host of such ancient worthies, . . . he may well afford to treat all cavillers, high or low, with a quiet curl of his lip. I need only add, that the shooting of game birds, over pointers and setters, has been, time out of mind, the *gentleman's* amusement; so much so, that I would hardly hesitate to make some guess concerning any man's antecedents, who should cross a stubble with me one of these crispy, brown October mornings. (7)

The book is intentionally mundane and didactic. Much of the material is copied, with acknowledgment, from works by Dr. Egbert B. Johnston, Col. William Stockton, and Henry William Herbert, a prolific contributor to the *Spirit of the Times,* to whom the volume is dedicated.

However serious his aim might have been, Hooper nonetheless lets flashes of his personality shine through, as when he lashes out at those who would misname and/or mishunt the quail.

The *Quail* is our chief, most reliable game bird in this section. A brave fellow he is too, and worthy to be properly known and called by his own true name, and not by his universal misnomer, *Partridge.* Let all true sportsmen call him aright—leaving it to the pot-hunter who shoots the bevy as it huddles on the ground, or murders the whistling cock on the fence or stump, and the clown who nets or traps what he cannot fairly kill, to apply to him a name for which there is no owner on this continent. Every one who writes on sports of the field has his rules; and *my* RULE THE FIRST is—*Call Quail, QUAIL!* Persistently give him his true name, and you are, young reader, one step nearer sportsmanship than the *commune vulgus* who kill him foully and serve him *more* foully, to wit: in hog's lard. . . . (9)

A few pages later, he lectures his readers on hunting terminology in the same spirited tone: "a dog is said to *quarter his ground,* NOT 'to hunt about the field'; he *breaks his charge,* and does *not* 'jump up and run after the birds.' " Gentleman Jonce continues in this fashion, returning like a good teacher to review the previous lesson: "My young readers will remember my *Rule the First: Call Quail, QUAIL!"* If partridges congregate in *coveys,* and a quail should never be called a partridge, then quail cannot be said to congregate in *coveys.* Although he allows some leeway on this point of terminology, Hooper nonetheless stands firm: "I know that far better sportsmen than I am, habitually use it; but it is a custom we should 'reform altogether.' My *Rule the Second,* then, is: *Call a Bevy of Quail, A BEVY OF QUAIL!"* (12)

Even lower than the boorish or ignorant hunters in Hooper's esteem are the "pot-hunters," who hunt for food rather than for sport. Here he denounces these unsportsmanlike quail-netters with the same degree of scorn he had once reserved for the dishonest land speculators who swindled the Creeks:

It is a practice which . . . will continue while gentlemen sportsmen treat those who are guilty of it as anything else than pot-hunting vaga-bonds. I do not mean that all who indulge in the villainous practice are worthless characters—though a majority of them are—but that the thing itself is so vile an outrage upon all sportsmanship, humanity, and magnanimity, that no man who *knows better* ought to countenance his best neighbor if he will not discontinue it. (60)

It is difficult—and probably unfair—to apply the standards of literary criticism to *Dog and Gun.* It represents Hooper's attempt to make a name in a genre—or perhaps two genres, the outdoor book and the gentleman's manual—very different from the tales of Simon Suggs and the yarns of Old Kit Kuncker. If Hooper once lost an election for being *"too d——d knowin' about Suggs to be honest himself,"*[3] in this work he strikes the pose of a gentleman qualified to instruct younger gentlemen in a gentle sport, with his ability to identify another gentleman by the way he "crosses a stubble" on a morning's hunt. The gentleman observes certain rules and customs ignored by the contemptible "pot-hunter" and quail-netter, *"commune vulgus"* (literally, "common mob"). Just as the gentleman does not write strictly for money, so does he not hunt strictly for food.

Critics have only been able to guess how much of Hooper's intent in writing *Dog and Gun* was to make readers forget Simon Suggs, and the little volume certainly did not do so. It did, however, enjoy a modest success, being reprinted in 1856, 1858, 1860, 1863, and 1871.[4]

Hooper himself announced in the *Mail* on February 3, 1857, the book's availability in Montgomery, as well as his debt to "our friend," William T. Porter, "for his valuable attention and kindness in reading the proof sheets of our bantling."[5]

Pistols at Ten Paces

In early 1857, with *Dog and Gun* published and the state elections not yet heated up, Hooper had time to travel and relax, although he did send accounts of his journeys back to the *Mail.* In May, Henry Coyne, the "Junior" editor, wrote that "The scribe of the 'Mail' has sought the Gulf shore, where he will soon be luxuriating for a brief 'spell' in the salt-water baths and breezes, inhaling the perfumes of magnolia and orange groves, and—eating pompano!" He continued, hoping Hooper's friends in Mobile will

guard against his overdoing the thing—(one pompano at a meal, if you please!) . . .

Be cautious, JONCE! It isn't often you get out from home, and there are several very wicked persons to be found on all sides of, and not far from, the intersection of Dauphin and Royal streets, and a "right smart sprinkling" of the same elsewhere about town.[6]

This bit of teasing is typical of the relationship between Hooper and Coyne, as they frequently exchanged good-natured jests. That next winter, for example, Hooper twitted Coyne about receiving an elaborate Valentine from an anonymous lady in New Orleans.[7] Later he noted that his bachelor partner, occasionally referred to as "our juvenile associate," "is certainly crinoline-struck in Columbus."[8]

Hooper's vacation in Mobile, however, was cut short when he rushed home to confront a rival editor, in the best tradition of the frontier journalist. He had responded to an editorial by Dr. N. B. Cloud, who had taken P. H. Brittan's place as editor of the *Montgomery Advertiser.* More precisely, Hooper answered an attack on him made by "The creature employed by Dr. N. B. Cloud, to edit the Montgomery Advertiser."[9]

Cloud's paper had in turn characterized Hooper's reply as having "tortured" out a meaning, "which none but a desperate opponent, regardless alike of truth and the intelligence of the public could discover."[10] The irate Hooper challenged Cloud to a duel and repeatedly demanded in the *Mail* that Cloud retract the statement. Cloud did not do so, stating that he knew no reason why he should "name a time and a place, beyond the limits of this State," and that he would "not accept a challenge to fight a duel on such grounds."[11] The affair gradually died down, but not before it had provided much entertainment for the readers of both papers.

Magnum Opus

Hooper had been a Mason for ten years, since March 20, 1847, and early in 1857 he applied his satirical talents to his fraternity. With other members of the Grand Lodge of Alabama he formed the "University of Comus," consisting of thirteen "choice spirits" within the Alabama Masonic organization. Each of these members was to write a humorous essay, for a satire on the ceremonies of Masonry. The contributors included A. B. Longstreet, noted author of *Flush Times in Alabama and Mississippi;* Charles Farrar Browne ("Artemus Ward"), well-known comic lecturer; George H. Derby, army officer and humorist; and actor Edwin Forrest. Hooper, elected "Zenon, the Grand Secretary of the University," wrote chapter 9, "The Thirteen Sages of Antiquity Caricatured."[12]

The book is a strange one, filled with symbolic drawings and allusions to secret rituals. Although the brief essay is inscrutable to one uninstructed in Masonic mysteries, the biographical essay by the book's anonymous editor (the volume was copyrighted in 1884 by one Robert Morris) is enlightening. "The writer made his acquaintance in the Masonic Grand Lodge of Alabama in 1857, and spent a week in his society there." After mentioning Hooper's membership in the original "tredecim" of the Order of Comus, the editor eulogizes him:

The satire of Mr. Hooper was exquisite. His conversation sparkled with keen points. Conventional platitudes and pretentious and sentimental claims were ruthlessly plowed under by the share of his sarcasm. If his wit at times was coarse, it, at least, was not circus wit, operatic wit, or what passed thirty years since as newspaper wit, but glowed with originality. His *bon mots* are yet the local currency around Montgomery. . . . In the brilliant coterie of southern humorists Johnson J. Hooper will ever rank among the foremost.

Amid the pro-forma references to Hooper's conversational charm and his good standing among southern humorists, the apology suggests one of the problems Simon Suggs caused his creator.

The biographical note also provides a rare glimpse of Hooper's attitude toward his journalistic responsibilities:

"But the grind of the political press," as he complained to us in 1857, "took the starch out of him," and the man designed by nature to be the comic historian of Alabama was "condemned by poverty to the setting up and knocking down of partisan politicians."

Apparently Johnson, in spite of the tradition that he lamented his early humorous ventures, also had moments when he regretted abandoning the "circle of 'jolly good fellows' " for the dog-eat-dog world of a political newspaper editor.

Once More into the Fray

Hooper had no leisure for innocent fun like *Magnum Opus,* however, for it was election time. On the state level, the Know-Nothings and Whigs were able to mount no organized opposition to the high-riding Democrats. With no party or candidates to endorse, Hooper had to be content with denouncing the perpetrators of the "Kansas Swindle" and commenting caustically on the "loathsome and discordant ingredients" of the Democratic national party in the *Daily Mail* for July 3, 1857:

> Eyes of Toombs, toe of Van
> Heart of fogy Bucha nan,
> Foot of Cobb, nose of Cass,
> Ears of Old Virginia's Ass—
> (4, col. 1)

When these ingredients were "thrown together into the political cauldron," the "idolators at the Democratic altar" would see "purified, a perfect statesman," according to the sardonic poem Hooper attributed to the *Columbus Enquirer.*

The Alabama Democrats were split between the "conservative" wing of the party and the "radical" Southern Rights wing. Conservative judge A. B. Moore defeated insurgent William F. Samford. Hooper had directed his editorial fire against those Democrats who would attempt reconciliation with the "Free Soil Northern Democratic Party," but in vain; his time had not yet come. Locally, his friend Thomas J. Judge, running as a "State Right Whig," lost to Democrat James F. Dowdell in spite of Hooper's editorial support. According to historian A. B. Moore, "The election of 1857 marked the disappearance of all organized opposition to the Democrats."[13]

But Johnson J. Hooper was undaunted, writing that "Those who manage [the *Mail*] have been in minorities during all their political lives; they therefore are not likely to shrink from opposing majorities." He further announced: "The position of the 'Mail,' politically, is a most decided *Southern Rights American Paper.*" [14] And, as his former attachment to the Union weakened, he replied to a pro-Union piece in the *Nashville News:*

If the above paragraph . . . means any thing, it means that the Union is worth more than the Institution of Slavery. On *such* terms, the Lord forbid that we should be Union men. And even to remain in the Union, with ceaseless aggression and insult from the North, is a little too much, we should think, for any man who has Southern blood in his veins.[15]

A Brief Respite

The *Mail* had been so successful that in the fall of 1857 Hooper and Coyne purchased new type. P. H. Brittan, formerly of the *Montgomery Advertiser* and now editor of the *Montgomery Daily Messenger,* praised the *Mail*'s appearance—"It is pretty now, but it well be *very* pretty when it gets into that bran-new suit of type"—as well as the partners' knack of making money. "Go on, brothers Hooper & Coyne—for in the bright lexicon of the Mail there is no such word as a small circulation—there are thousands of names in its bright lexicon of an address book."[16] In addition, they acquired another partner, when John F. Whitfield bought part interest in the *Mail* in the winter of 1858. Whitfield took over much of the day-to-day writing, which had been weighing on Hooper.

Also during this period, Mrs. Hooper, Adolphus, and William were able to move to Montgomery. In the *Daily Mail* for March 31, Hooper thanked "several kind ladies" who brought "corn hoe-cake[s] and butter-milk" by way of welcome.[17] (Typical of the fog shrouding Hooper's personal life, this contradicts other accounts that the rest of the Hooper family had joined Johnson in late summer of 1855.)

With the political front temporarily quiet, Hooper devoted more space to gentler subjects—books, theater, wines, etc.— sparing no superlatives in his praise of things southern.

He again found time for literature, as he prepared for publication a series of historical essays by General Thomas S. Woodward, many of which originally appeared in the *Daily Mail.*

These nostalgic recollections of the early days in Alabama consisted primarily of Woodward's letters to Hooper, Edward "Horseshoe Ned" Hanrick, historian S. J. Pickett, F. A. Rutherford, and John Banks. The book version, *Woodward's Reminiscences of the Creek, or Muscogee Indians, Contained in Letters to Friends in Georgia and Alabama,* was published in January 1859.[18] Hooper contributed the sober introduction, honoring the General. He boosted the work as beneficial to Alabama and liberally bestowed free copies. The volume was favorably received by critics, and the *Daily Mail* noted on March 17, 1859, that it "has been eagerly sought for and only a few copies remain on sale" (1, col. 2). By November 30, he noted that they were "all sold."

As a token of his appreciation for Hooper's editorial efforts, the General mailed him two centipedes and a tarantula from Texas. Hooper acknowledged them in the *Daily Mail* on April 16, 1859 (1, col. 2), "The 'specimens' were living, but not in very good condition, and we were constrained to end their lives, which, however, we did as pleasantly as possible to them— with the best alcohol."

On March 9, 1858, "the Junior" had noted in "Editor Estray" that Hooper "abruptly broke from the ranks of the Can't-get-away Club" to travel to Washington City by way of North Carolina (1, col. 1). In the nation's capital his old friend "Horseshoe Ned" Hanrick showed him about the town on foot and introduced him to such notables as General Lewis Cass and Senator Sam Houston. Hooper recorded his observations and impressions for the *Mail*'s readers.

Michigan's Lewis Cass, about whom he had had little good to say in the past, he found to be a "remarkably hale, and, apparently, active, though very stout, old gentleman," whose conversation exhibited "a directness, coupled with great energy of expression about him, which we greatly admired." After asking Cass about General Walker, whose efforts to colonize Nicaragua had been cheered by southerners and opposed by northerners, Hooper concluded the audience: "Fearing to bore the General, we incontinently left, after breathing the atmosphere of greatness . . . , but without getting the Austrian Mission."[19]

He complained about the government, about the

inaccessibility of the "servants of the people" in high places. . . .
many declare that it is easier to obtain audience of a head of a department under the British Government than under this. "Messengers"
guard the passages and "pocket" visitors in ante-chambers, where they
often remain until their ardor cools and then withdraw in despair.
. . . But the aristocracy of office is thoroughly established at Washington, and will no doubt grow more and more exacting, until the present
metropolis shall hold the capitol of neither the North nor South. How
long it shall be before that consummation is reached, is for the South
to say.

And, ever the gentleman, he found fault with the manners
of his countrymen: "It is a fact, we believe, that the Southerners
at Washington are not very courteous to the antislavery men."[20]
The accounts had appeared somewhat belatedly, as Coyne
noted in the *Daily Mail* on March 31 (1, col. 1): "Our Senior
has been too unwell, since his return, a few days ago, to write
out some loose notes of men and things in Washington. . . ."
The illness, Coyne noted, was "the acutest pangs of rheuma-
tism," and in mid-July Hooper went to Talladega, seeking relief
in the mineral waters. Coyne teased: "he will not, in consequence thereof, be able to participate in the pleasures of the
ball-room with his accustomed ease and gracefulness, but a little
exercise in that way will no doubt benefit him materially."[21]
He returned yet again to Talladega in the summer, but his
health was still worse in the fall, when Coyne announced on
September 13 (1, col. 1) that Hooper, "whose general health,
we regret to say, has been in the decline for some time—has
gone to the country to recruit his health and regain his
strength. . . ."
While Hooper was gone, William T. Porter died, on July
15, 1858. The *Daily Mail* simply reprinted an obituary from
the *New Orleans Picayune.*[22]
Hooper was feeling better soon after, for a report on the
Montgomery Fall Races turned up in the *Spirit* for November
13, 1858 (27:475). Most noteworthy are his references to failing
eyesight, his inability "to trace the lines he scrawls hereon."
After Porter's death, T. B. Thorpe and Edward E. Jones co-
edited the *Spirit.* Carried away by nostalgia for the good old
days, the "Flush Times," as it were, Hooper wrote of

the "Old Spirit" as the single remaining link which bound us in kindly feeling and sympathy to New York—as the sole relic of an era of cordial association and genuine mutual esteem—. . . . For the love of the "old times," and for the memory of old friends, let us rally to the aid of the glorious old "Spirit."[23]

Chief among the "old friends," William T. Porter, the one man most responsible for Hooper's literary success, had died eight months earlier, his death barely acknowledged by his old friend Johnson J. Hooper.

Thorpe welcomed "Number Eight," listing him among the *Spirit*'s correspondents on February 12, 1859 (29:1), and later (February 26), announcing wishfully that "Among those who have 'spoken out in meeting' and 'made a clean breast of it,' is our old friend 'Simon Suggs,' who comes to the rescue, with saddlebags full of specie, and a heartful of 'sympathetic offerings' " (25). As it turned out, however, Hooper had time to do little more than report a few horse races.

In the winter of 1858–59, Hooper made two forays into the ore-rich mountains of Tennessee, singling out on March 5 the Ducktown Copper Mines, subject of a story copied from the *Charleston* [South Carolina] *Mercury.* A week later, notices in the *Daily Mail* explained everything: An organizational meeting of the Alleghany Mining Company was proposed to purchase and work certain mines and mining properties in Ducktown, Polk County, Tennessee. Hooper was elected secretary, and William Lowndes Yancey was listed as a supporter. Subsequently, Yancey was elected chairman.[24]

The *Mail* makes no further mention of the Alleghany Mining Company. Apparently the investors needed to buy 5,500 shares for $550,000 and that purchase was not forthcoming.[25] We can only surmise whether the long shadow of Simon Suggs had fallen over the enterprise.

Over a year later, however, Hooper would have the last laugh, albeit a rueful one, as he recalled the Ducktown venture in the pages of the *Daily Mail* for April 21, 1860 (2, col. 3). It seems that after the project "fell through," the most valuable part of the property passed into the hands of "some New Orleans gentlemen who formed a company and are now working the mine." The mine, it turned out, was now "the richest in the

world." Hooper had words for those investors who had hung
back: "What an escape (from wealth,) our nibblers had *that
time!*"

The *Montgomery Mail* continued to prosper, having landed
the contract for the city and post-office printing. Typographical
and other improvements brought praise from the *Pensacola* [Flo-
rida] *Gazette:* "This fine sheet . . . is now one of the best-printed
and edited papers in the South."[26]

The State Elections of 1859

Returning home from a trip to Mobile and New Orleans,
Hooper threw himself once more into the political wars, although, more than ever before, he was truly a man without a
party. He found one candidate to back, however: William F.
Samford, a Southern Rights Democrat running against the conservative regular party candidate, incumbent governor A. B.
Moore. Hooper also went further than ever before in his support
for William L. Yancey, who was stumping the state on behalf
of Samford. Yancey was also active in the formation of Leagues
of United Southerners, which had as their purpose the disruption
of the Democratic party and the uniting of the southern people
into a sectional party. Hooper supported the Leagues, and Yancey, sensitive to criticism that they were too heavily laden with
Know-Nothings, "claimed that the *Montgomery Mail* was the
only American paper which was supporting the League." [27]

Again Hooper was disappointed. Samford was beaten badly,
with 18,000 votes to Moore's 47,000. "National Democrats
carried every district in the state," [28] Alabama voters demonstrating their faith in that party's ability to defeat the "Black Republicans." They hoped it would save the South and protect slave
property.

The burden of partisan politics temporarily lifted from his
shoulders, Johnson had time for horse racing, as shown by some
of his contributions to the *Spirit.* Equestrian honors piled up
for him, as a South Carolina major named a race horse, "Jonce
Hooper," in his honor, and he was elected secretary of the
Montgomery Jockey Club.

In October he journeyed to New York City, heralded by
editorial fanfare from Thorpe in the *Spirit:* " 'Col. Simon Suggs,'

or rather our friend, Johnson J. Hooper, Esq., . . . has been spending a few days in this city. . . . Mr. Hooper, as our friends generally know, is . . . an honor to the press, of which he is a distinguished member."[29]

Little is known of Hooper's trip to New York, although a note in the *Spirit* for October 22, signed "Alabama," praised the Fifth Avenue Hotel and its "crowds from Georgia, Alabama, Mississippi, and Louisiana" (29:439). For whatever reasons, and it is not difficult to imagine why a true son of Alabama might have felt ill at ease in such a Yankee stronghold, he was back in Montgomery by the end of October.

Hooper's Increasing Hostility toward the North

Although he professed his attachment to the Union for as long as he could, the rise of abolitionist sentiment in the North brought about a corresponding increase in Hooper's sectional loyalty. As he sought out things southern to praise, so he also began to seek out things northern to condemn.

On October 22, 1855, for example, the *Daily Mail* ran "A Big Brothel—A Peep into the Bowers of Free Love" (2, col. 2), apparently Hooper's digest of a "country editor's" visit to New York City, where he attended a meeting of a Free Love Society, sort of a house of prostitution where "Passional Attraction," rather than money, was the currency. After dwelling with scandalized fascination on the "hellish sensuality" of the beautiful damsels who have "submitted to the embraces" of the *"philosophers,"* those "male devils," Hooper concluded:

Can we wonder, that in a society where such elements as these exist, abolition vagaries should be produced! A society which submits to the existence of such an association, even on the most limited scale, in its midst, must be depraved to its inmost core. Such we believe is New York—a very "Sea Sodom—Gehenna, of the Waters!" We can only look for destructive principles and action, social and political, where such infinite and ineffable impurity has found a "local habitation and a name."

Just as northern writers and readers drooled over the sexual implications of slavery (according to H. Montgomery Hyde,

Harriet Beecher Stowe's *Uncle Tom's Cabin* was avidly read by "devotees of the lash"[30]), so southerners missed no opportunity to link sexual and other immorality with the baffling moral aberration of abolitionism. A few months later, he would state that "all abolitionists are by nature or the operation of their principles, made liars, thieves and cowardly murderers."[31]

In "Wholesale Seduction—Boston Morals," in the *Daily Mail* for November 26, 1856 (3, col. 1), Hooper used a story of "immorality" in a Boston girls' school to point out the Yankees' hypocrisy:

It would seem . . . that the saints of that city are not altogether free from those carnal weaknesses which their romances are inclined to saddle almost exclusively on slaveholders. In fact, from the developments of the article mentioned, it is very apparent that "the Flesh and the Devil" "hold their own" among the descendants of the Mayflower Pilgrims, quite as fully as among the warmer regions of the South. . . .

That is a nice little kettle of fish, for pious, puritanic, nigger-loving, psalm-singing Boston! It would be difficult to parallel such detestable pollution in the lowest sinks of rotten and rotting London.

Southerners were not about to forget that the ancestors of their slaves were brought here on Boston vessels, and that Beacon Street was built with the profits from the trade in rum, slaves, and molasses.

"New England Morality," in the October 1, 1857, *Daily Mail* (1, col. 1), gives Hooper's reaction to a *Boston Post* report that "a temperance professorship is needed at Cambridge for the benefit of some college officers." The facetious Alabamian favored the idea, for he had long been of the opinion that the teachers from the "abolitionized" New England colleges were drunk when "they exhibited their open, but hurtless and effeminate hostility to the constitutional rights of the South." He hoped that "the freedom-shriekers" would contribute to a temperance fund, so that "the South may thereby rest forevermore, from the maledictions and slanders of inebriated college teachers."

The economic system of the North came under Hooper's fire in "Free Bread," from the November 12, 1857, *Daily Mail* (1, col. 1). The senior editor pointed out with satisfaction that telegraph reports indicated a "Hungry Mob" in New York was menacing the mayor and threatening to sack the subtreasury unless the members of the mob obtained relief. "There's *free* society, for you," gloated the defender of slavery.

Like so many other southerners, who felt themselves increasingly beleaguered by the fanatical North, Hooper was highly sensitive to criticism of anything southern. In January 1855 he had met with and written favorably of actor Dion Boucicault. On Wednesday, December 21, 1859 (2, col. 3), however, he lauded T. B. Thorpe's unfavorable review of Boucicault's *The Octoroon,* a play written "to pander to anti-slavery feeling": "**Thorpe,** in the criticism, speaks like the true Southern man he is. . . . **Boucicault,** we are sorry to see, like hundreds of others who have received the hospitality of the South, has shown himself, at last, a dirty, ungrateful little dog."

A typical editorial, "Hang the Seditious," left no doubt as to what should be done to northern visitors or immigrants who attempted to "slip about among the plantations, endeavoring to corrupt the slaves. . . ."[32] A brief notice in the *Daily Mail* for February 3, 1857 (2, col. 1), declined an ad for the *Philadelphia Saturday Evening Post* as "unfit for Southern circulation."

By the end of the decade, the intransigent South increasingly refused to do business with the North. Hooper copied a story from the *Philadelphia Ledger* lamenting the economic hardship caused by the boycott with the heading, "**We Devoutly Thank God!**"

It rejoices our soul to hear of this early justice. Every howl of the North West wind will bring sweet dreams to us, for we shall know that it is pinching the thin-clad limbs of some at least of those who would place the knife at our throats, if they could. . . .

"Workmen discharged," eh! And "particularly trying at this period of the year"—is it? It was not "particularly trying," was it, to send thousands of broad blades to Virginia, to put into the hands of our loyal slaves, for the purposes of rebellion and massacre! Oh, no! And the Hartford man, too—he has discovered an "unfriendly feeling," has he? Didn't suspect it, from what happened at Harper's Ferry—not he![33]

Persistent references to Harper's Ferry, site of John Brown's "raid," indicate that southerners felt physically threatened by the North's zeal. In the *Daily Mail* from 1859 on, recurring mentions of "free-soil vermin" and headlines like "More Abolition Rascality" were interspersed with notices of the meetings of the "Mounted Rifles," the "Metropolitan Guards," and the Montgomery "True Blues." As early as June 15, 1857 (2, col. 1), "Young America in Arms" had reported with approval the parade of the "City Rangers," a new, voluntary military corps of "lads of about 12 to 14 years of age."

Further evidence of the South's sense of being trapped by a hostile government controlled by the North may be seen in the *Daily Mail* for February 3, 1860 (2, col. 2), written on the occasion of Pennington's being elected speaker of the national House of Representatives: "He is one of those who believe the African to be the equal of the Anglo-Saxon; . . . the unrelenting North forced him down the throat of the humble, imbecile South." Throughout the South, journalists of Hooper's conviction, although not often of his skill, were whipping up their readers to the point where the election of a Republican president, with the attendant threat of economic and social chaos, was unthinkable and unendurable.

The Calm before the Storm

During the early months of 1860, as the nation breathlessly—or breath*fully,* considering the vast amount of windy rhetoric on both sides of the Mason-Dixon Line—awaited the party nominating conventions, Hooper was busy boosting the culture, economics, and overall superiority of the South in general and Alabama in particular, with the sort of articles on mining, railroads, theater, etc., that had characterized the *Mail*'s pages since its inception. The "rejuvenated" paper now sported new type and a masthead engraving of the state capitol.

The *Spirit* announced on February 18, 1860 (30:13), that "our friend Johnson J. Hooper, Esq., one of the most popular editors in the South," would be covering the New Orleans and Mobile races and urged "our friends to award to 'Col. Suggs' all the honors he deserves as a gentleman." Soon after, on March 6, the *Daily Mail* wrote that Hooper was embarking on "a series of rambles" to report on railroad progress for the *Mail* and other papers (2, col. 2). He attracted even more attention than usual: The *Mobile Mercury* hailed the "inimitable Jonce Hooper, of the Montgomery Mail, . . . which is now one of the largest and most readable papers in the South. . . . Aside from his ability as a writer, the world does not contain a better nor a braver heart than throbs in the bosom of J. J. Hooper."[34] While in Columbus, Mississippi, he saw that the *Columbus Democrat* had copied the Charleston *Mercury*'s story designating him a major. Hooper acknowledged in the *Daily Mail* for March 31 (1, col. 3): "so I am a Major of Mississippi Militia to the end of the chapter, or until the next war. . . ."

In New Orleans the *Crescent* welcomed him as "the Southern author and humorist, the immortal chronicler of the sayings and doings of 'Simon Suggs' and the editor of the Montgomery *Mail.*"[35] Other papers throughout the South greeted him with approbation, perhaps none so warm as that of the *Atlanta Confederacy:*

the Mail has won an enviable reputation, in the noble cause of Southern Rights, and we cannot but admire the bold stand which the senior editor, J. J. Hooper, Esq., has taken in behalf of the South. Pinning his faith to no party, or politician, Hooper, has entered the arena, determined to do battle, to the bitter end, in defence of the South.[36]

In recognition of his status as a capable and widely traveled southern journalist, Hooper was constantly asked about the future of the South. As the *Daily Mail* for April 21 put it (2, col. 2), "The fate of the Slave States" would be determined at the forthcoming National Democratic Convention, because that "convention is the only body carrying with it sufficient moral power to commit any party or section to a proper defence of the constitutional rights of slavery."

As this poem from the *Weekly Mail* shows, however, he pinned little hope on the convention:

The South

Men of the South! look up,
   There are omens in the sky;
The murky clouds are gathering,
   Red Meteors flash on high;
And there are moans and mutterings

> Sent up by heaving waves;
> Our eagle poises on his wings
> And shrieks o'er patriots' graves.
>
> . . . .
>
> Men of the South! take heed—
> Be watchful and be firm;
> Ye have to smite the giant's head
> And crush the poisonous worm.
> Arrayed around your chartered right,
> Strong in your holy cause,
> Be this your cry in valor's fight:
> Our State—Our Rights—Our Laws![37]

Melodramatic though the verse is, it shows how the southern press was rushing headlong down the road to secession and war.

The Election of 1860

By 1860 the differences within the Democratic party could no longer be reconciled. At their convention in Charleston in April, the pro–(Stephen) Douglas majority attempted to skirt the slavery issue by adopting a platform plank abiding by the decision of the Supreme Court regarding slavery in the territories. Southerners led by Alabama's Yancey demanded a guarantee that the federal government would protect slavery in the territories. When they did not get it, Yancey and the Alabama delegation bolted the convention, followed by most of the cotton-state delegates. Thus disrupted, the convention was able only to adjourn, with plans to reconvene in Baltimore in June.

Editorially, Hooper hailed the news as "one of the most important passages in History," rejoicing in the "announcement of 'issue joined' between the enemies and friends of the institution of African Slavery."[38] Earlier he had urged his readers: "Stand by Yancey! . . . with but one political pledge—that we shall stand by the South, her interests and her honor, *come what will!*—we go on our way, trusting that all our friends will consider themselves at liberty, in this our birth month. . . ."[39]

When the national Democratic party met again in Baltimore in June, the moderate Douglas delegates who controlled it would at first admit only their allies. Even their compromise position excluded the rebellious Alabama and Louisiana delegations. The "bolting" of the Charleston convention was repeated, led by Yancey and Alabama. As a result, there were two Democratic conventions: the northern one, which nominated Stephen A. Douglas; and the southern one, which nominated Kentucky's John C. Breckinridge.

Meeting in Chicago, the Republicans passed over well-known abolitionist William Seward to nominate a skillful but obscure politician named Abraham Lincoln. To this free-for-all was added a fourth candidate, Tennessee's John Bell of the Constitutional Union party, newly formed of Know-Nothings, old-line Whigs, and dissident Democrats.[40]

Johnson J. Hooper was not among these. Although he had for a time in early 1860 supported the shortlived Southern Rights Oppositionist party, with "Minute Men" clubs, which were formed to declare "to the *world* that we *will not* submit to the control of a Black Republican as President of the United States,"[41] he immediately and enthusiastically embraced Breckinridge as his candidate. Hooper cut short a trip to New York and arrived in Baltimore just in time to hear Breckinridge accept the seceders' nomination.

At last, Hooper had found a candidate who embodied his Southern Rights principles: "Can any true and loyal Southern man hesitate a moment to decide that Breckinridge and Lane are the ticket that demands his support?"[42] Yancey's advocacy of Breckinridge certainly strengthened Hooper's resolve. Hoole writes: "If Yancey was the orator of secession, Hooper was its journalist."[43] The editor of the *Mail* passionately attacked those he considered the enemies of the South:

Mr. Douglas is to come and speak for us in Montgomery. . . . He could hardly do less. He has spoken of the *clam-bakes* of New England and stated his preference for that species of bivalve, over Southern negroes. It is right that after praising clams so strongly, he should now come and give the "nigger" his share.[44]

Nor did he hesitate to attack local disloyalists, as he accused J. W. Taylor of being "personally disloyal to the South" in the *Daily Mail* for October 26, 1860, and refused to retract the allegation.[45]

In addition to covering pro-Breckinridge speakers, Hooper

traveled to Ashland, Kentucky, to hear his man speak. The senior editor of the *Mail* made his position clear: "Friends, stand by us, as we intend to stand by you and 'sink or swim' *with the South!*" Some days later he went further, stating that, in the event of Lincoln's election, "the only hope for Slave States, is instant secession. . . ."[46]

On the eve of the election, he counseled brave actions, naively underestimating the severity of the Union's response and predicting a rosy future for the seceding states:

Men of Alabama! we have only to be firm, to find safety. If (in case of Lincoln's election,) we secede, we shall do so with the wealth of a great nation in our depots and in those of the other Seceding States. There will be no war and, after a few weeks, no distress. Our cotton bales are the bond which obligates the armies and navies of Europe to defend us. They form the subsistence of our enemies, themselves. They cannot exist without them. They must come to us for them, on their very knees, instead of with arms in hands. We have only to be true to our own sense of right, to obtain Security and Prosperity!

He closed with a plea for unity:

Shall not our people unite, then, under such circumstances? The political differences of the past—supposing Lincoln elected—ought to be buried among Southern men. We mean, of course, all true hearted men of the South, who only desire the welfare of their country and section. *After this day,* there is no cause for dispute among us. We can be, if we choose, one people; and we ought to be, and must be. . . .

Let Southern Union be the word![47]

The Die Is Cast

The worst fears of Hooper and the South were soon realized. He saw from the early election returns that the cause was lost and wrote in the *Daily Mail* on November 7 (2, col. 1): "It is enough for the present to know that the North is determined, if we submit, to wipe us from the face of the earth. The details by telegraph would cost us a sum of money which we cannot conveniently lavish for such news."

What the final tally would show was that the Republicans' northern strategy had been successful. While collecting barely 40 percent of the popular vote, they had carried every northern state, plus the two western ones of Oregon and California, amassing 180 electoral votes. Breckinridge carried the South for seventy-two electoral votes, while Bell picked up Tennessee, Kentucky, and Virginia, which had thirty-nine electoral votes. And the northern Democrat, Douglas, while polling half a million votes fewer than Lincoln and half a million more than Breckinridge, got only the dozen electoral votes of Missouri and New Jersey.

It was time for Yancey, Hooper, and the other secessionists to make good their word. Hooper reminded his readers on November 10 of a meeting "to deliberate on the condition of the South in the present crisis of affairs. Come one, and all, the enemy is at our gates, let us prepare to meet the danger" (2, col. 1).

Soon the governor declared December 24 as the date for the election of delegates to the Secession Convention, to be held on January 7, 1861. Hooper displayed the names of Yancey and Thomas H. Watts as "Secession Nominees," and crossed rifles appeared at the top of the *Mail*'s news columns. In addition to printing fiery editorials, Hooper was one of five members of the "Committee of Correspondence" of the "Central Committee of Safety," a secessionist body of which Yancey was but one prominent member.[48]

When the Alabama State Convention convened on January 7, the crowd was so enthusiastic that the legislative chambers had to be cleared. The press was excluded, too, and so Hooper waited outside with the rest. Impatient, on the eleventh he flew an Alabama flag, borrowed from the river steamboat *Le Grande*, from the *Mail* offices.[49] Later that day the word went forth that the Ordinance of Secession had been adopted.

Not until later would it be known how close the vote had been: sixty-one in favor, thirty-nine against, with the "Cooperationists," the conservatives of non-slave-holding northern Alabama, losing out to the radical secessionists of the Black Belt.[50] So bitter had been the debate that Yancey had intimated that those who opposed the Ordinance would be "dealt with as traitors," to which a northern delegate replied that "Yancey might come at the head of any force he could muster, but 'we will meet him at the foot of our mountains, and there, with his own selected weapons, hand to hand, face to face, and settle the question of the sovereignty of the people.' "[51]

But all these doubts and differences were laid aside in the jubilation of the moment, as Mrs. A. G. Walker, wife of the chief justice of the Supreme Court, fired a cannon in salute to the new Republic of Alabama, and the city went wild with celebration. Hooper expressed the feelings of the Secessionists in the *Mail* on the twelfth:

Te Deum Laudamus! And so, all hail! to the glorious, free and independent Flag of the Sovereign Republic of Alabama! Forever may it wave in honor over a happy, chivalrous, united people. And to that sentiment, we know, that all our "people say Amen!"[52]

Chapter Seven

In Service of
Alabama and the South

One Nation, Divisible

Early 1861 was a tumultuous time throughout the nation in general, but especially so in Alabama. On January 4, even before the secession vote, state troops had seized forts Morgan and Gaines in Mobile Bay and the federal arsenal at Mount Vernon, at the order of Governor Moore. While the southern states were seceding, plans such as the Crittenden Compromise were debated in Congress, but were doomed to defeat by hard-liners on both sides.

After the parades and fireworks of secession day had subsided, Alabamians were once again divided over which course to take. Some looked upon secession as a bargaining ploy to gain a more equitable arrangement within the Union. Northern Alabamians were unwilling to forget their hostility to the leaders of the "Black Belt" (Yancey was burned in effigy in the northern county of Lawrence) and talked about merging the counties of northern Alabama with those of southeastern Tennessee to form a new state, "Nick-a-Jack."[1]

Events, however, rushed inexorably on. Tension mounted between the state of South Carolina and the garrison of Fort Sumter, in Charleston Harbor. Some northern leaders called for the outright freeing of the slaves, while still others said the South should be allowed to go in peace. Buchanan vacillated during the last days of his term, and Lincoln subsequently postponed a decision on Fort Sumter until April.

All Alone

During the excited days before the convention, Hooper's editorial responsibilities were multiplied by the absence of his

partners: Ill health had required Henry Coyne, "the Junior,"
to repair to New Orleans and Mobile. John F. Whitfield, who
at twenty-four was junior even to "the Junior," had enlisted
as a second corporal in the Montgomery "True Blues" and
was stationed near Pensacola, Florida.[2]

"All Alone!" lamented Hooper, informing his readers that
"the entire charge of the 'Mail' has devolved on its senior editor,
who happens not to be remarkably robust." For one man to
perform all the editorial duties single-handedly, he went on,

. . . is an occupation not much more pleasant than that of the man
on the tread-mill, with only about equal honor and emolument.

These facts stated, we trust that our readers, *in this dark time before
the perfect dawn of Independence,* will make reasonable allowance for
the deficiencies which they detect.[3]

To fill the pages of the *Mail,* Hooper "cut and pasted" pieces
from other papers and printed dispatches off the telegraph
wire.

Serving the South

Meanwhile, representatives of the seceded states were to meet
in Montgomery on February 4, to organize the Confederate
States of America. So bitter had been the secession controversy
in Alabama that virtually none of the legislators or other prominent leaders such as William L. Yancey was represented.[4] When
the meeting convened, in the senate chamber of the Alabama
capitol, the delegates from Alabama, South Carolina, Florida,
Louisiana, Georgia, and Mississippi elected Howell Cobb of
Georgia permanent president. W. P. Chilton of Alabama then
nominated for permanent secretary "Johnson J. Hooper, . . .
a gentleman too well and favorably known, to render it necessary
for me to say anything about his ability and qualifications, for
the proper discharge of the duties of that office."

Robert Toombs of Georgia moved that the nomination be
made by acclamation, and the galleries erupted in such enthusiastic applause that President Cobb insisted that "all manifestations
of approbation should be, for the future, discontinued."[5]

As Marion Kelley puts it, "on February 4, 1861, 'Jonce
Hooper received the reward—the only one he ever received—
for his loyalty to the South."[6]

The *Spirit of the Times,* predictably, saw all this as a chance for some fun at the expense of

The celebrated Jonce Hooper, author of the sides-shaking "Simon Suggs," which everybody ought to read, Senior Editor of the "Montgomery Mail," which everybody does read, undisputed owner—in fact monopolist of one of the uglist [*sic*] phizes which everybody, forewarned, tries hard not to see—the selected and admitted rival in personal pulchritude of the rail-splitting and repulsive Abraham Lincoln; being elected, by acclamation, Secretary of the Southern Congress, approached the desk to take his seat. The insensate desk as if for the nonce, imbued with sense and nerve, at first seemed to sway, and swerve, and shudder, at the approach of the hideous Jonce, but, by and by, grew firm and still, and quite submissive to the gallant "Quill." . . . Jonce is unquestioned "pumpkins" in a peculiar way, and bore the honor of his appointment with becoming modesty and dignity. . . .[7]

Accustomed though Hooper was to jokes about his looks, we can imagine his reaction to being compared to Abraham Lincoln.

Tongue in cheek, the editor of the *Spirit* defended its former Alabama correspondent in the same issue (49). Another eyewitness, however, untutored in the waggish ways of gentleman journalists, wrote quite matter-of-factly that "The Southern Congress has met, Howell Cobb of Georgia presiding and Simon Suggs of Montgomery clerk."[8] Try as he might, Hooper could not live down Simon Suggs.

In anticipation of his new duties, the *Weekly Mail* announced on February 8 that the senior editor would probably have little to do with the paper for some weeks. During this period of partial withdrawal he had occasion to note his disapproval of some editorials in the *Mail,* and on February 12, 1861, the *Daily Mail* stated that "Mr. Hooper, senior editor of the *Mail,* is not now engaged in furnishing copy for the paper."[9]

At the same time, his duties had increased. In addition to recording the long and involved proceedings of the Congress, he was later charged with arranging for "the publication of the Provisional Constitution for the Government of the Confederate States of America, with the Autograph Signatures of the Members of Congress." The list of his tasks was soon enlarged to include the editing of "fair copies of all acts passed by Congress," and a "full index for the same."[10]

In addition, when Leroy Pope Walker was elected Secretary of War, he hired Hooper as his "Private Secretary," a position that made Johnson a "staff officer of the Confederate States Army." Faced with the urgent pressures of the impending war, Walker and the War Department had overwhelming responsibilities with a volume of correspondence to match. Much of this correspondence was handled by Hooper between March 16 and the extra session of the Congress convened by President Jefferson Davis on May 21. According to Kelley, "His letters were not important; they were clearly those which could be safely trusted to an underling." [11]

Scarcely a month after he had announced he was no longer writing for the *Mail*, he sold his interest in the paper to one Robert Frasier. He was leaving for good the career he had followed since he was twenty-seven. Amid the dispatches telling of the bombardment of Fort Sumter and Lincoln's call for Union Army volunteers, the brief announcement was practically lost. The *Montgomery Confederation*, however, saluted the departure of "a witty, spicey writer, [who] will be very much missed by the readers of the Mail."[12]

In May the Provisional Congress authorized Hooper to hire additional clerical help, at six dollars per day. Further, he was named librarian of the Confederate Congress. Montgomery was astir during that time with the impending transfer of the Confederate capital to Richmond. Wounded civic pride spurred the Alabama papers to protest the change and to deny that Montgomery was liable to contagious diseases or any other shortcomings, but in vain. On May 21, 1861, the Congress passed an act specifying that the government should be moved to Richmond in time for the next congressional session on July 20. The resolution bore the signature of one of Alabama's most loyal sons, "J. J. Hooper, Secretary for the Congress."

With little time for reflection, Hooper had to prepare to leave Montgomery, whence he had come fifteen years earlier to make his mark in the world, a city he had championed in the pages of the *Montgomery Mail*, perhaps its most illustrious newspaper. He would leave his home city, his family, and friends to serve his beloved South in her new capital, Richmond, Virginia. As Kelley writes,

To Alabama he had come to watch the Indians leave; now he was watching lines of grey men leave. . . . This man—this complex, intense human—left Alabama; he never saw again the red hills of the Creek country, the swerve of the Alabama in the bend opposite Montgomery, the flow of men down Market street into the square and out again through Commerce street. He never again met legislators on Goat Hill; he never again argued at the Exchange; he was gone to Virginia.[13]

Gone to Virginia

When Johnson J. Hooper reached Richmond in late May 1861, he found a city whose population of 40,000 had nearly tripled due to the sudden influx of politicians, soldiers, merchants (both legitimate and otherwise), and numerous others brought to the old city by the war and the subsequent establishment of the Confederate capital there. It is a shame that Simon Suggs could not have joined this throng, presenting as it did such abundant opportunities to a man of the Captain's abilities.

The Secretary of the Provisional Confederate Congress had no time for such idle speculation. In addition to his secretarial duties, he was also charged with many of the details of setting up shop for the new government. The former editor of the *Montgomery Mail* was not lost in the shuffle, however, as the *Richmond Daily Dispatch* welcomed him on June 10:

Among the strangers now in our city, we have been most happy to meet Johnson J. Hooper, Esq., . . . the brilliant orator and wit. . . . Mr. Hooper is Secretary of the Southern Congress and is equally admired for his genius and humor, and for the sterling qualities of the high-toned gentleman. "Simon Suggs," if Mr. Hooper had never produced anything else, would alone immortalize him.

As W. Stanley Hoole comments, "Once more, alas, the Shifty Man had gotten there first . . ."[14]

In spite of the intense competition for lodging at wartime prices, Hooper was able to find rooms in the respectable Richmond House, temporary home of other officers of the Congress. Mary Hooper and their younger son, Adolph, joined him. William, by now seventeen years old and a second lieutenant in the Confederate Army, remained in Montgomery. In late October Hooper wrote to his older son one of the few letters of his that survive:

My Dear Son:

You don't know how solicitous I am about you: not about your personal safety, for that a soldier must risk, but about your habits, moral and intellectual. There was never a true soldier to whom his honor was not dearer than life; there was never a great one, who was not *a student.* For your own sake and that of your name, read diligently military books and observe closely details, in every army as you have opportunity; and above all, learn to spell. You can not imagine how important it is. You could never make a respectable Adjutant without this homely accomplishment. Whenever you doubt about the spelling of a word, refer to a Dictionary and *not* Webster's if you can get any other.

You will have many temptations to dissipation; you will often feel like indulging a lazy fit; these are the sirens which destroy the promise of hundreds of brilliant young men.

But above all, my Son, remember that *Truth* is the foundation of all fame and honor—of all that is desirable in life. The liar (I don't fear *your* being one,) is always a coward, morally at least.

We are all in pretty good health. Your mother was very uneasy about you, till I telegraphed. She now anxiously awaits a letter.

Your Ma was delighted to hear, by Tom, of your being put on Col. Maury's Staff—but *has* a Colonel a Staff? If so, what post is yours?

Give my regards to Col. Maury and to Rice and Yancey. I hope you will all have a chance for glory ere long.

Your Ma and Dolph send love. Write at once.

Your affectionate father,
J. J. Hooper[15]

In addition to giving a rare glimpse of the personal warmth and devotion to family that are often mentioned by his family and contemporaries, this letter is filled with the senior Hooper's concern for courage, integrity, and the other hallmarks of a gentleman's character.

In the spring and summer of 1861, Richmond was filled with excitement fueled by a series of easy victories beginning with the Union abandonment of Fort Sumter on April 14. Tempted by the proximity of Richmond and the rapidly expiring ninety-day enlistments of their militia, the Union mounted a July offensive that culminated in their being routed at Bull Run (Manassas) on July 21. For the South, these were very costly victories, in that they reinforced the prevailing opinion that the war could be won in a few months and that the Yankees could not fight.

Lincoln and the North, on the other hand, settled down to fight a long war, in which their superior manpower and resources could be brought to bear in conjunction with the "Anaconda Plan," whereby the South was to be encircled by naval blockade and western offensives and slowly strangled to death.[16]

All that was in the future, however, a future that Johnson J. Hooper would not live to see. In the brief flush of prosperity before ruinous wartime inflation set in, the city was flourishing as Richmond enjoyed the social season of 1861–62, "as gay and expensive as ever one had been before the war."[17] When his arduous duties permitted, he partook with his wife and son of the advantages of the city, walking about the streets or lounging in the fashionable lobby of the Richmond House.

For the conviviality and conversation of masculine companionship, Hooper turned to the venerable and prestigious Powhattan Club, modeled along the lines of the old London gentleman's clubs of Shakespeare and Ben Jonson's time. Among these "gifted and accomplished men of letters, lawyers, doctors, clergymen and philosophers in every range of human thought," Hooper the celebrated raconteur was in his element. An 1891 account of the Powhattan Club lists the distinguished newcomers brought to Richmond and the club by the war, concluding: "and by no means least, J. J. Hooper of Alabama." This same account, by H. D. Capers, recalls how his yarns "flowed with great ease of expression in apt and expressive language." His anecdotes were better than any the members had previously heard, and his conversation contained "much that was solid food for the mind, well prepared and served in such a manner as to insure the physical and intellectual being against the possibility of dyspepsia in any form."[18]

About this time, perhaps with some premonition, Hooper's mind turned to thoughts of religion. His detractor William Garrett to the contrary, Hooper had never been an irreligious man. Descendant of an Anglican Divine and a Congregational minister, he was an Episcopalian, the faith in which his sons were baptized, and had devoted space in the *Mail* to Montgomery's churches. Nevertheless, old friends from Alabama and new ones were surprised by the intensity of his sudden immersion in the Roman Catholic faith, guided by Father Robert Hayne Andrews of St. Peter's Cathedral, and by his subsequent joining, appar-

ently on December 7, 1861, of the Catholic Church. He carried
with him a Catholic prayer book and would recite prayers, sometimes in Latin, to friends. To his death he remained a devout
Catholic and saw much of his new friend, Father Andrews.

Simon Fights the Tiger

The easy optimism of the previous spring was waning by
early 1862, as the casualties and the shortages mounted. On
February 16, a Union general named Grant captured strategic
Fort Donelson, on the Cumberland River in Tennessee, along
with nearly 15,000 Confederate soldiers. A long and bloody
battle at Shiloh in Tennessee cost the South 4,000 dead, including General Johnston. Little consolation that Northern casualties
had been heavier.

Meanwhile, the Confederate leadership was having problems,
some the result of clashing personalities, others the result of
political principles. According to twentieth-century historians,
Jefferson Davis was quite unsuited to the office of president.
Inexperienced in administration, he prided himself on his military judgment and therefore interfered incessantly with his gen-
erals. Vice-President Alexander H. Stephens hated Davis and
"made a fetish of state rights." Indeed, precisely the insistence
on states rights that had led the Southern states to secede made
it increasingly difficult for the Confederacy to muster the growing numbers of men and amounts of materiel needed to with-
stand the Union juggernaut.[19]

The early signs of unrest did not cause the Confederacy to
change its top leadership, as in November 1861 Davis and Stephens were reelected for a "permanent" six-year term. Changes
in Congress and the cabinet, however, were numerous. Hooper's benefactor, Leroy Pope Walker, was replaced by Judah P.
Benjamin as secretary of war. Robert Toombs, the man who
a few brief months ago had moved that Hooper's nomination
for secretary of the Provisional Congress be made by acclamation, had resigned as secretary of state after an argument with
Davis, and his post had not yet been filled.

The Provisional Congress itself was abolished in February
in favor of a permanent two-house legislature. Hooper's job
as secretary was snatched away from him. Suddenly cut adrift,

he struggled to come about. But his years of antagonizing the "bogus democrats" left him with little sail for tacking into what Hoole describes as "the wind of ruthless political patronage."[20] On February 18, 1862, he stood for election to the secretaryship of the Senate. Against four opponents he survived until the sixth ballot, losing by one vote to James H. Nash. The two houses having elected their secretaries on the same day, there was no chance for him to obtain the secretaryship of the House of Representatives, which was won by a former assistant secretary of Hooper's.

When the now "permanent" administration staged its inaugural parade on Washington's Birthday, marching through the miserable winter drizzle from the Hall of Delegates of Virginia to the statue of George Washington, Johnson J. Hooper was not part of the procession. The man who had left his home and sold his business to serve his beloved South had been cast aside.

Playing Out the String

Mary and Adolph having been forced to return to Montgomery some time before, Hooper was now alone in Richmond, bereft of his position, which, for all its arduousness, had paid $2,500 per year. Fortunately, his friend Howell Cobb, former president of the Provisional Southern Congress, was now in charge of editing and publishing the proceedings of that body, as well as the constitutions of the Confederate States of America. Hooper already had these documents, and therefore he was the logical person for the job.[21]

Assured of employment, though less prestigious than that of congressional secretary, Hooper set to work. Before he could even begin to organize the vast accumulation of papers, however, he was stricken with a serious illness, apparently tuberculosis. During his last two months he lay bedridden at the Richmond House. Far from his home and family, he was not alone: Father Andrews sat with him daily, and friends came frequently and brought mail from home. Capers recalled: "Ah! Well do I remember our vigils at his bed-side, the sweet gentle words of love to those who were watching the death of the vital spark, the calm great sleep of his noble spirit."[22] Talk was of the Yankee campaign against Richmond. At the beginning of June, General Robert E. Lee was placed in command of the Army of Northern Virginia. Lee and General Stonewall Jackson would defend Richmond so brilliantly and with such daring that the South would have new hope—for awhile.

Johnson J. Hooper, however, would not live to see those victories, or the ultimate defeat. On Saturday, June 7, 1862, two days before his forty-seventh birthday, he died, giving "up to God," as the *Richmond Enquirer* put it, "as noble a soul as beat in human breast. Peace be with him—his memory with us!"[23] His friend Father Andrews administered the last rites.

On a rainy ninth of June, he was buried in an unmarked grave in Hollywood Hill's Shockhoe Cemetery, among the already numerous Confederate dead. Fittingly, still other soldiers were rushing out of the city to still other battles. Wrote his friend Capers: "There we laid his body away, where the murmuring waters of the James will sing for him a requiem while time shall endure."[24]

His obituaries, like that of the *Richmond Enquirer,* quoted in part above, were full of praise:

With sincere sorrow we have to announce that Johnson J. Hooper died at the Richmond House, in this city, on Saturday evening late, after an illness of a few days. Mr. Hooper was widely known as an author, journalist and public official, and not only to our particular profession, but to the literature of the South, his loss is very serious. At the time of his death he was arranging to complete some work which would have been of immense value to the independent literature of our country.[25]

The balance is devoted to his religious conversion.

To the *Richmond Daily Examiner* he was "an excellent man, full of genial qualities, and respected by all who knew him."[26]

Not for a week after his death did word reach Montgomery. His old friend Henry E. Coyne, now "the Senior," draped the *Mail* in black and wrote:

Few men have ever lived of more genial impulses and warmer affections . . . he never stopped to consider the sacrifice to himself if he could serve a friend. The past year has deprived every community of some of its best loved, but of the many who have fallen in war or by diseases, few will be more severely regretted, or longer remembered, than Johnson J. Hooper.[27]

Chapter Eight

Johnson J. Hooper
in Retrospect

Poor and Neglected?

Because of Johnson J. Hooper's versatility, any estimate of his stature must take into consideration his public as well as his literary achievements. As a champion of an impressive list of lost causes—the Creeks, the Whigs, the Know-Nothings, the Southern Rights Oppositionists, and the Confederate States of America—he certainly elicits sympathy, if not downright pity. One is tempted to accept the epitaph from the otherwise flattering biographical note in *Magnum Opus:* "He died poor and neglected at the tail-end of a lost cause," [1] and pull out a handkerchief. However, Hooper's own sense of humor, as well as his accomplishments, precludes any such overreaction. At the time of his death, he was certainly not wealthy, but neither was he neglected.

Although he was elected state solicitor of the "Bloody Ninth" Circuit and later secretary of the Provisional Confederate Congress, perhaps Hooper's greatest nonliterary achievement was editing the *Montgomery Mail*. And here, journalism being a relation, even if a poor one, of literature, his preeminence owed something to his fame as the creator of Simon Suggs as well as to his lively (and often powerful) writing style and his sense of composition. As numerous flattering editorial references quoted throughout this work will attest, "Jonce" Hooper was the "beau ideal" of the southern newspaper editor in the mid-nineteenth century.

Garrett and the Democrats: "The Constant Trailing of the Slow-Track Dog, from Whose Fangs There Is No Final Escape"

If there are any blots on Hooper's escutcheon, it is William Garrett who put them there. Not only did he provide for posterity the picture of Hooper huddled in his green blanket coat, humiliated by being called to answer to the name of Simon Suggs, but he also branded him as one who "had never tended to a very moral course of life, and the subject of religion seemed never to have entered his thoughts, or at least never had any perceptible influence on his conduct." Garrett apparently took great satisfaction in pointing a bony finger at Hooper, to "let him stand as a beaconlight, to give warning of the rock on which the manly ambition and hopes of his youth perished."

Garrett's antipathy to Hooper might result from any of a number of factors, not the least of which is his apparent sympathy with the Temperance movement and Hooper's with "convivial habits," to which, by the way, Garrett attributed Hooper's relatively early death.[2] Second, Garrett was a Baptist and Hooper was nominally an Episcopalian, although he was not a regular churchgoer. And Hooper's conversion to Catholicism was perhaps not the one for which Garrett might have hoped. In his *Reminiscences* he notes with alarm that Simon Suggs's "art, in the perpetration of fraud, [in "The Captain Attends a Camp Meeting"] was greatly assisted by the cant and hypocrisy of a pretended piety and church membership!"

Further, Garrett was a prominent Democrat and had served as Alabama secretary of state and as speaker of the state House of Representatives. Hooper, as we have seen, had been an editorial gadfly to the "bogus democracy" for most of his journalistic career. (Garrett writes that Hooper "first edited the 'Whig' *or some paper of like politics* [italics mine] in East-Alabama." He had tirelessly assailed the national Democratic party for its "softness" on questions of slavery and free-soil, from the Kansas-Nebraska Act right up to the eve of secession. In a typical editorial in the *Daily Mail* on September 15, 1857, he rejoiced that "the *young men* of the Democracy begin to leave the rotten

hulk of National-Democratic Freesoilism" (1, col. 1). Lewy Dorman writes: "Hooper was probably the most able of the Whig
editors. He combined wit and force in his writings and his attacks
on the Democrats were highly effective." [3]

All questions of party loyalty aside, one has to wonder if,
when Garrett was composing his entry on Johnson J. Hooper,
he was recalling an otherwise forgotten editorial from the *Daily
Mail* of many years ago, on July 20, 1855, entitled: "JUDGE
SHORTRIDGE AND EX-SPEAKER GARRETT." During the election campaign, Hooper had defended his friend and candidate,
George D. Shortridge, against the Democrats' and the *Advertiser*'s attack on his bank indebtedness by pointing out that "Years
ago, Col. William Garrett . . . while receiving a salary from
the State, availed himself of the benefit of the general bankrupt
low [*sic*]. On this schedule, we have been informed, was a debt
due by him to the State Bank or one of its Branches." Garrett
had continued to accept his salary, and "no paper opposed to
him politically, ever printed a word to his disparagement concerning it. Col. Garrett prospered in life, and we have no doubt
paid the debt he thus owed the State" (2, col. 3). Doubtless
he did, and Col. Garrett certainly paid back tenfold the "debt"
he owed Johnson J. Hooper. The creator of Simon Suggs might
have lived well, but Garrett's living longer proved the best
revenge.

Although it is impossible to prove such conjecture, it seems
plausible that in subtle ways Baptist-Democratic influence had
a hand in tarnishing the luster of Hooper's reputation, especially
in state and regional politics, where he so desired to shine.
Many accounts of Alabama history before and during the Civil
War make no mention of him at all. While Dorman and Hoole
(the latter's prejudice as Hooper's biographer is understandable)
credit him with extensive journalistic influence, such writers
as A. B. Moore, Jr., author of *The History of Alabama,* deal
with him only as the author of *Simon Suggs.* Moore names Democrat William F. Samford as "probably the most notable States
Rights penman in the South." [4]

Despite its wide circulation, Garrett's account should be taken
for just what it is: a political opponent's recollections published
ten years after Hooper's death. There is much other testimony
to establish the good character of Johnson J. Hooper. His rela-

tives and others hailed him as a warm and loving father and family man in general. Others recalled him as "The Champion of the Creeks." [5]

In addition to references in history books, another index to Hooper's importance is the legion of powerful and influential men who called him "friend." His good friends were widespread and numerous, with William T. Porter of the *Spirit of the Times* perhaps the best known and certainly the northernmost. In the South he counted among his friends and acquaintances Alabama humorist John Gorman Barr, "Omega,"; fiery secessionist orator William Lowndes Yancey; poet A. B. Meek; historian Albert J. Pickett; industrialist Daniel Pratt; political leaders Thomas Hill Watts, who became governor of Alabama, and Thomas J. Judge; Confederate Secretary of State Leroy Pope Walker; thespian-humorist Sol Smith; and many editors in Alabama and elsewhere.[6]

His editorials dealt not infrequently with morality and the public good. He promoted the arts and helped secure a theater for Montgomery. In addition to condemning high prices and public executions, he once held forth on "The Morality of the Country," lamenting the way in which society damns the petty scoundrel and welcomes the great one: "It is this false tone of public opinion which emboldens bad men of decided capacity to venture on stupendous swindles. It is all of a kind with the morality which gives such men as Barnum social position—and it is all terribly wrong." [7] The message is the same as that of the Suggs tales, but, unfortunately for American literature, Hooper had chosen to express his indignation in the openly didactic form of the newspaper editorial.

Johnson's sense of decency was also offended by what he considered to be breeches of social decorum, as evidenced by "Outrageous," inspired by an incident during an appearance of Campbell's Minstrels:

We understand that, for two or three evenings, a person living in this city has carried to the Campbells' entertainments a woman of the town and seated her in the vicinity of ladies. The Manager, of course, cannot be expected to know all these people, but the gentlemen who observed the fact should have caused the removal of the parties.[8]

The "gentlemen" evidently failed to fulfill their obligation to shield the "ladies" from such a "woman of the town."

This concern with the privileges and obligations of a gentleman runs throughout his life and writings. He at one time lamented that "the Southerners at Washington are not very courteous to the anti-slavery men." In reporting on the Montgomery Jockey Club, of which he was secretary, he asserted that the members were "gentlemen of the highest social position and unimpeachable honor." [9] To defend his own honor, he was once ready to fight a duel with Dr. N. B. Cloud, of the *Montgomery Advertiser.* And *Dog and Gun* was primarily intended to instruct young gentlemen. Recall that Gentleman Jonce "would hardly hestitate to make some guess concerning any man's antecedents, who should cross a stubble with me one of these crispy, brown October mornings." Similarly, his letter to his son demonstrates great concern that the young Hooper behave and live properly.

Beneath this apparent concern and authority, though, one wonders if there might be a bit too much protestation, a bit of whistling in the dark (if, indeed, a gentleman whistles other than to his pointer). Is there a wistful undertone to Hooper's kidding of recent Democratic converts after their victory in the state and national elections of 1856? "They feel it is 'we' who are successful—. . . who beat the Know Nothings—*and who have the right of admission into the 'good society' in Montgomery* [italics mine]." Could it be that, in spite of his ancestors, the Anglican Divine and "The Signer," Johnson J. Hooper, who owned no slaves and little property, who could barely afford to establish his family in Montgomery, felt a little uneasy among the elegant planters and other aristocrats of Montgomery and the Black Belt?

An editorial in the *Daily Mail* for November 27, 1855, lambastes the "Cow Heel Aristocracy," those of

low origin and contemptible pretensions. In a republican country, there should be no aristocrats—no class to be rated superior to another, by the law, or by custom. . . . But if we are to have an aristocracy *at all,* let it be an aristocracy of birth and blood—let it not be the base counterfeit of a contemptible original. Any aristocracy but the "COW-HEEL." . . .

The *"Cow-heel,"* (which bases its pretensions on its wealth,) is the most arrogant and insolent of all aristocracies. For the good of this class, there ought to be a *"Pedigree of our Great Families"* published annually. (2, col. 2)

Thus, Hooper argued, a wealthy merchant, son of a cobbler, would not be allowed to assume superiority to a carpenter. Or, one might extrapolate, to the grandnephew of a signer of the Declaration of Independence.

Ironically, Hooper's sentiments echo those of his great-uncle William Hooper, who reportedly said in 1776: "I am indeed afraid that when independence shall have been achieved, talents and virtue may be thrown into the shade, and the mob may govern." [10] Little wonder if Johnson became impatient watching the advancement of men inferior to him in birth and ability.

In Johnson there is something of his father, Archibald Maclaine Hooper, that intelligent, well-meaning man who failed in all his practical pursuits. While he was by no means incompetent, legend has it that Johnson was no genius as a financial manager. Recall his humorous pleas to advertisers and subscribers to pay their bills. It was with the addition of Henry Coyne that the *Mail*'s financial situation was bettered. They frequently improved the *Mail*'s equipment and physical plant to enhance the paper's appearance and profitability.

Yet, he did attempt to get ahead, to prosper above and beyond his editor's salary. In 1859 he and Coyne bought a lot in Montgomery. Also, he arranged in 1859 to be the agent for Audubon's *Birds of America* in Alabama.[11] Perhaps his closest brush with wealth was the ill-fated Alleghany Mining Company venture, in which Hooper could not find backers to purchase what later proved to be one of the richest copper mines in the world.

He took after his father not only in his knack for not getting rich, but also in his fatal weakness for belles lettres, which reputedly impeded Archibald's legal career. And, we may surmise, the long shadow cast by the shifty Captain Suggs to some degree blighted his creator's career in public life.

Hooper's Literary Reputation

Though he would have wished otherwise, Johnson J. Hooper's main claim to fame is his humorous writing, especially *Adventures*

of Captain Simon Suggs. Tradition has it that no less a notable
than William Makepeace Thackeray, Hooper's contemporary
and one of the greatest English novelists of the nineteenth century, pronounced him "the most promising writer of his day." [12]
The prominent southwestern humorist Joseph G. Baldwin paid
Hooper the compliment of writing "Simon Suggs, Jr., Esq., a
Legal Biography," which appeared in his *Flush Times in Alabama
and Mississippi.*

A random sampling[13] turns up such assessments as that of
Joel Campbell Dubose, who wrote in 1908 that "Johnson Jones
Hooper had a mind very much like that of Baldwin. He ranked
high as a serious journalist and advocate. His recognised abilities
made him secretary of the Confederate Congress, and yet his
fame rests upon the rollicking humor of his *Adventures of Captain
Simon Suggs. . . .*" Like so many other writers, however, Dubose
returns to Hooper's fabled repudiation of the Suggs tales: ". . .
a work of which he was heartily ashamed as he rose in public
esteem." [14] More recently, Rhoda Coleman Ellison praises "the
stories of Johnson Jones Hooper, which in the forties reached
the high-water mark of Alabama journalistic humor. . . ." [15]

And Eugene Current-Garcia, in detailing the personal and
editorial relationship between Hooper and William T. Porter,
declares: ". . . the spark that kindled the *Spirit*'s brightest blaze
of Southern humorous stories was lit by Hooper. . . ." [16]

Hooper's Literary Influence

Hooper's influence on later writers provides further demonstration of his importance. Not surprisingly, that influence may
be found in his adopted state of Alabama, as Benjamin Buford
Williams sees evidence of Hooper and Suggs in the works of
minor writers Idora Moore and Francis Bartow Lloyd ("Rufus
Sanders").[17]

Hooper is also listed among the southwestern humorists influ-
encing more recent, better-known writers. In "Southwestern
Humorists and Ring Lardner—Sport in American Literature,"
for example, Christian Messenger compares Hooper and other
southwesterners' satirical, distanced treatment of the frontier
folk with Lardner's vernacular handling of bored suburbanites
and oafish athletes.[18] Similarly, "Faulkner and the Southwestern

Humorists," by Cecil D. Eby, mentions Hooper in the company of other southwestern humorists whom William Faulkner transcends, even while sharing with them certain regional and folk concerns. Further, "Flem Snopes is cut from the same cloth as Simon Suggs."[19]

M. Thomas Inge gives Hooper less credit, pointing out: "How much Faulkner assimilated from growing up in the same environment that earlier nurtured the southwestern humorists, and to what extent he actually read and imitated the humorous writings, is a moot question, but he did cite Sut Lovingood as one of his favorite fictional characters."[20]

Perhaps the most easily demonstrable instance of Hooper's literary influence is the case of his near-contemporary Mark Twain. Born in Missouri in 1835, twenty years after Hooper, Samuel Langhorne Clemens grew up in a frontier America similar to Hooper's. As various critics have noted, his attitude and art were shaped by a background he shared with the southwestern humorists, a background that included the oral tales of the frontier and even the works of the southwestern humorists themselves.

Possibly the most direct argument for Hooper's influence on Clemens is the inclusion of an 1845 edition of *Some Adventures of Captain Simon Suggs* among the volumes in Clemens's vast library.[21] Also, he selected "Simon Suggs Gets a 'Soft Snap' on His Daddy" for *Mark Twain's Library of Humor,* published in 1888.[22]

Kenneth Lynn asserts: "Twain's unpublished notebooks reveal that such books as *Georgia Scenes, Flush Times, Simon Suggs,* and *Major Jones' Courtship* were personally familiar to him [Twain]." [23]

Several critics have pointed out incidents in Mark Twain's writing that seem to bear the stamp of Jonce Hooper. Bernard De Voto in *Mark Twain's America* cites the strong resemblance of a scene in chapter 20 of *Huckleberry Finn,* in which the Duke and the Dauphin dupe a camp-meeting congregation, to "The Captain Attends a Camp Meeting." Indeed, De Voto finds that Mark Twain "falls below his predecessor," and that the scene is "all but identical" with "The Captain Attends a Camp Meeting." Although De Voto finds Hooper lacking in the "Olympian detachment" of Mark Twain, which relegates his sketch to a "lower level," the realism of Hooper's piece is "sharper, its intelligence quite as great, and its conviction considerably greater." He feels that Mark Twain would have done well to have followed his model more closely. And, in a footnote, he calls attention to the "amusing" similarity of the dogs' names: Aunt Hetty's Bull Wilkerson in "Taking the Census" and Bull Harbison in *Tom Sawyer.* [24]

John Rachal's "Scotty Briggs and the Minister: An Idea from Hooper's Simon Suggs?" compares the encounter between homespun Scotty Briggs and the learned and high-spoken minister in *Roughing It* with "Simon Plays the 'Snatch' Game." Both rely on a failure to communicate and the gambling metaphors employed by the less-educated character. Rachal also cites the imagery of Simon in the camp-meeting chapter, in which he "has come in on *narry pair* and won a *pile,*" as "a somewhat rougher parallel." He concludes by saying that "the idea of a communication breakdown between cardsharp and minister does not occur frequently enough in Southwestern humor to attribute the parallel to Mark Twain's borrowing a standard motif from frontier literature generally."[25]

Other intriguing parallels exist. As mentioned above, the motley crowd of courthouse-square loafers in "Jim Bell's Revenge" presages those in *Huckleberry Finn,* although Mark Twain's view of this subspecies of homo sapiens is even darker than Hooper's. Hooper's "Col. Hawkins and the Court" also provides another similarity to a scene in chapter 21 of *Huckleberry Finn,* in which Col. Sherburn shoots old Boggs, both in the setting and the detached, ironic style with which it is presented: "Here it must be remarked, that the town was particularly populous *in the dog way*—if that be not a solecism—and Jim being aware of the fact, had provided himself with a hunting horn, an instrument on which he was a most capital performer." [26]

"A Requiem While Time Shall Endure"

Johnson J. Hooper is assured of a place in history. As we have seen, partisan politics did much to reduce this place to a footnote in the history of Alabama and the South. Unfortunately, his early death and his premature turning away from humorous writing did much to relegate him to a similar place in American literary history. Just as the incoming Democratic tide in state and regional politics washed away most traces of Hooper's public service, so the tide of national literary humor that flooded the regional backwaters of Down East and Old Southwest alike seriously eroded his literary reputation. The "Literary Comedians," platform lecturers such as "Mark Twain," "Artemus Ward," "Petroleum V. Nasby," "Josh Billings," and others, applied many of the southwestern humorists' techniques on a broader, national scale.[27] Today, the very quaintness of mispronunciations, malapropisms, misspellings, and phonetic transcriptions of dialect that once made the southwestern humorists and literary comedians alike so funny makes their writings an almost inaccessible foreign language to subsequent generations of casual, impatient readers.

Within the subgenre of southwestern humor, however, Hooper has a secure niche in the history of American literature. As one of the very best of those gentlemen humorists, with only George Washington Harris ranking indisputably above him, he shares an important place in the development of modern American literature. With the others, his emphasis on comic realism and vernacular style helped pave the way for Samuel Clemens, Ring Lardner, William Faulkner, Erskine Caldwell, and, less directly, for many others who would dominate the mainstream of American literature in the late-nineteenth and twentieth centuries.

Most of all, he will be remembered for Simon Suggs, that backwoods Barnum who managed time and again to "come in on *narry pair* and [win] a *pile.*" As long as Americans seek new countries in which to be shifty, Simon will be there, with "a hand of cards in [his] fingers and one in [his] lap."

Notes and References

Chapter One

1. All biographical information, unless otherwise cited, comes from W. Stanley Hoole, *Alias Simon Suggs; The Life and Times of Johnson Jones Hooper* (University, Ala., 1952); *Adventures of Captain Simon Suggs*, ed. and intro. Manly Wade Wellman (Chapel Hill, N.C., 1969); and Marion Kelley, "The Life and Writings of Johnson Jones Hooper" (M.A. thesis, Alabama Polytechnic Institute, 1934).

2. Fanny Hooper Whitaker, "The Hooper Family," *North Carolina Booklet* 5 (July 1905):45–46.

3. Hoole, *Alias,* p. 10.

4. Ibid., p. 8.

5. *The Widow Rugby's Husband, A Night at the Ugly Man's, and Other Tales of Alabama* (Philadelphia, 1851), pp. 125–34.

6. *Adventures of Captain Simon Suggs,* pp. 65–66.

Chapter Two

1. *Some Adventures of Captain Simon Suggs, Late of the Tallapoosa Volunteers; Together with "Taking the Census," and Other Alabama Sketches.* By a Country Editor (Philadelphia, 1846), pt. 1:149–64; pt.2:165–68. Hereafter referred to by page numbers in the text.

2. For more on the southwestern humorous tale in general, see Walter Blair, *Native American Humor* (San Francisco, 1960), pp. 62–101; Hennig Cohen and William B. Dillingham, eds., *Humor of the Old Southwest* (Boston: Houghton Mifflin, 1964), pp. ix–xxiv; M. Thomas Inge, *The Frontier Humorists; Critical Views* (Hamden, Conn., 1975); and Franklin J. Meine, ed., *Tall Tales of the Southwest* (New York, 1930).

3. Blair, *Native,* p. 83.

4. In Hoole, *Alias,* p. 49; p. 201, n. 18, 19.

5. Eugene Current-Garcia, "Newspaper Humor in the Old South, 1835–1855," *Alabama Review* 2 (April 1949):113.

6. Milton R. Stern and Seymour L. Gross, *The Viking Portable Library American Literature Survey,* vol. 1: Colonial and Federal to 1800, revised and expanded (New York: Viking Press, 1968), p. 7.

7. Benjamin Franklin, *The Papers of Benjamin Franklin,* ed. Leonard W. Labaree (New Haven: Yale University Press, 1968), 12:134–35.

8. Blair, *Native,* pp. 337–48.

9. Ibid., pp. 62–63.

10. *Spirit of the Times; A Chronicle of the Turf, Agriculture, Literature and the Stage* 13 (December 23, 1843):505.

11. *Spirit* 14 (April 27, 1844):104.

Chapter Three

1. Blair, *Native,* p. 65.

2. Norris W. Yates, *William T. Porter and the Spirit of the Times* (Baton Rouge, 1957), pp. 17–22.

3. Cohen and Dillingham, *Humor of the Old Southwest,* pp. 388–89.

4. *Adventures of Captain Simon Suggs,* pp. 6–7. Hereafter referred to by page numbers in the text.

5. Hoole, *Alias,* p. 52.

6. In *Adventures of Captain Simon Suggs,* p. xvii.

7. Robert Hopkins, "Simon Suggs: A Burlesque Campaign Biography," *American Quarterly* 15 (Fall 1963):459.

8. Hoole, *Alias,* pp. 55–57; 202, n. 43.

9. Ibid., p. 203, n. 45.

10. James Parton, *Life of Andrew Jackson* (Boston: James R. Osgood, 1876), 2:319.

11. Blair, *Native,* pp. 91–92.

12. According to Ann Wyatt Sharp, Hooper spoke and wrote the "prestige dialect" of the Cape-Fear-Peedee River Valley. This is the language of Hooper's narrator and "is the same dialect from which Hooper considered that Simon and his companions deviated." "The Literary Dialect in The Simon Suggs Stories of Johnson Jones Hooper" (Ph.D. diss., University of Alabama, 1981), pp. 12, 17.

13. *Spirit* 15 (November 29, 1845):471.

Chapter Four

1. *Spirit* 16 (May 23, 1846):145.

2. In Hoole, *Alias,* pp. 65; 207, n. 22.

3. Kelley, "Life and Writings of Johnson Jones Hooper," pp. 62–63.

4. Ibid., p. 62.

5. Ibid., p. 63.

6. *Spirit* 19 (April 14, 1849):87–88.

7. Ibid., April 21, p. 100.

8. Ibid., July 7, p. 231.

9. *Adventures of Captain Simon Suggs,* p. 135. Hereafter referred to by page numbers in the text.

10. *Spirit* 19 (July 28, 1849):270.
11. Hoole, *Alias,* p. 208, n. 34.
12. According to ibid., four numbers of the *Tribune* survive.
13. *The Widow Rugby's Husband,* p. 97. Hereafter referred to by page numbers in the text.
14. Henry Watterson, "The Personal Equation in Journalism," in *The Profession of Journalism,* ed. Willard G. Bleyer (Boston: Atlantic Monthly Press, 1918), p. 99.
15. Henry Nash Smith, *Mark Twain of the Enterprise* (Berkeley and Los Angeles: University of California Press, 1957), pp. 38–39.
16. *Spirit* 19 (October 6, 1849):388–89.
17. Ibid., November 17, p. 460.
18. Ibid., November 10, p. 450.
19. *Adventures of Captain Simon Suggs,* p. 166. Hereafter referred to by page numbers in the text.
20. *The Widow Rugby's Husband,* p. 35. Hereafter referred to by page numbers in the text.
21. Bernard De Voto, *Mark Twain's America* (Boston, 1932), pp. 93–94.
22. V. L. O. Chittick, *Ring-Tailed Roarers; Tall Tales of the American Frontier, 1830–1860* (Caldwell, Idaho: The Caxton Printers, 1941), p. 15.
23. Cohen and Dillingham, *Humor of the Old Southwest,* pp. 16–25.
24. Blair, *Native,* pp. 374–80.
25. Mark Twain, *The Adventures of Huckleberry Finn* (New York: Bantam, 1981), pp. 134–35.
26. Ibid., pp. 135–36.
27. William Garrett, *Reminiscences of Public Men in Alabama* (Atlanta, 1872), p. 529. Garrett was not exactly an admirer of Hooper.
28. Benjamin Buford Williams, *A Literary History of Alabama; the Nineteenth Century* (Cranbury, N.J., 1979), p. 78.
29. Hoole, *Alias,* p. 176.
30. Ibid., p. 73.
31. Kelley, "Life and Writings," p. 187. In a letter to Kelley from Franklin J. Meine.
32. *Spirit* 20 (March 23, 1850):52.
33. Hoole, *Alias,* p. 215, n. 82.
34. Ibid., p. 77.

Chapter Five

1. Hoole, *Alias,* pp. 216, n. 3; 81.
2. *Montgomery Daily Mail,* December 6, 1854, p. 2, col. 1.

3. *Alabama Journal,* September 3, 1851, in Hoole, *Alias,* pp. 80; 216, n. 2.

4. John M. Blum et al., *The National Experience,* 3d ed. (New York: Harcourt Brace Jovanovitch, 1968), pp. 321–25.

5. Hoole, *Alias,* p. 217, n. 5.

6. Ibid., p. 81.

7. Kelley, "Life and Writings," p. 97.

8. Hoole, *Alias,* p. 81.

9. *Daily Mail,* December 7, 1854, p. 2, col. 2.

10. Ibid., October 25, 1855, p. 3, col. 1.

11. In Hoole, *Alias,* pp. 84; 217, n. 14. *Standard* reference from *Daily Mail,* December 12, 1854, p. 2, col. 1.

12. *Daily Mail,* January 22, 1855, p. 2, col. 2.

13. Ibid., November 20, 1854, p. 2, col. 2.

14. Hoole, *Alias,* p. 88.

15. Albert Burton Moore, *History of Alabama and Her People,* 3 vols. (New York, 1927), 1:273.

16. Ibid., p. 274.

17. *Daily Mail,* August 9, 1855, p. 2, col. 1.

18. Ibid., August 14, 1855, p. 2, col. 1; Hoole, *Alias,* p. 90. (Note that this contradicts other evidence placing his family in Montgomery in late 1854.)

19. Hoole, *Alias,* p. 92.

20. *Daily Mail,* September 10, 1855, p. 3, col. 1.

21. *Read and Circulate: Proceedings of the Democratic and Anti-Know-Nothing Party in Caucus; or the Guillotine at Work, at the Capital, during the Session of 1855–'56* (Montgomery, Ala, 1855), p. 4.

22. *Daily Mail,* March 3, 13, 1857, in Hoole, *Alias,* pp. 105; 224, n. 42.

23. Ibid., November 20, 1855, in Hoole, *Alias,* p. 92.

24. Hoole, *Alias,* pp. 92; 219, n. 42.

25. Ibid., p. 95.

26. *Daily Mail,* February 12, 1855, p. 2, col. 1, in Hoole, *Alias,* p. 220, n. 48.

27. Ibid., December 6, 1854, in Hoole, *Alias,* pp. 85; 218, n. 18.

28. Ibid., August 13, 1855, p. 2, col. 3.

29. Blum et al., *National Experience,* p. 325.

30. *Montgomery Tri-Weekly Mail,* June 7, 1856, in Hoole, *Alias,* p. 97.

31. Kelley, "Life and Writings," p. 113.

32. *Tri-Weekly Mail,* June 7, 1856, in Hoole, *Alias,* p. 97.

33. Blum et al., *National Experience,* pp. 322–25.

34. *Daily Mail,* March 5, 1857, p. 2, col. 3.
35. *Tri-Weekly Mail,* July 3, 1856, in Hoole, *Alias,* p. 98.
36. Moore, *History,* 1:275.
37. Blum et al., *National Experience,* p. 325.
38. Moore, *History,* 1:276.
39. In Hoole, *Alias,* p. 99.
40. *Daily Mail,* November 25, 1856, p. 2, col. 1.
41. Ibid., November 7, 1856, p. 2, col. 1.
42. [Johnson J. Hooper], "Old Mammy Halladay's Experience," *Spirit* 27 (May 30, 1857):183.
43. [Johnson J. Hooper], "In Favor of the Hog," ibid. Also in *Yankee Notions* 6 (September 1857):263. Text used is that of the *Spirit.*
44. *Porter's Spirit of the Times* 1 (September 6, 1856):14, in Hoole, *Alias,* pp. 100; 222, n. 21.
45. *Daily Mail,* November 12, 17, 1856, in Hoole, *Alias,* p. 101.
46. Ibid., November 22, 1856, p. 2, col. 1.
47. Ibid., December 10, 1856, p. 2, col. 1.
48. Ibid.
49. Garrett, *Reminiscences,* pp. 528–29.
50. Kelley, "Life and Writings," pp. 122–23.
51. Hoole, *Alias,* 223, n. 34.

Chapter Six

1. *Daily Mail,* December 24, 1856, p. 2, col. 1, and February 10, 1857, p. 2, col. 2.
2. *Dog and Gun; A Few Loose Chapters on Shooting, Among Which Will Be Found Some Anecdotes and Incidents,* in *Moore's Rural Handbooks* (New York, 1858). Hereafter referred to by page numbers in the text.
3. *Spirit* 19 (July 28, 1849):270.
4. Hoole, *Alias,* pp. 106; 224, n. 44, 49; 225, n. 50; 256.
5. *Daily Mail,* February 3, 1857, p. 2, col. 3.
6. Ibid., May 20, 1857, p. 1, col. 1.
7. Ibid., February 11, 1858, p. 1, col. 1.
8. Ibid., May 17, 1858, p. 1, col. 1.
9. Ibid., June 6, 1857, p. 1, col. 2.
10. Ibid., June 23, 1857, p. 1, col. 1–4.
11. Ibid.
12. *Magnum Opus. The Great Book of the University of Comus. The Pandect of our National Hilaritas, Comprising Essays upon the Thirteen Divisions of the Rituals; Sketches of the Tredecim Doges, Authors of the Plan, and a Monitorial Guide to the Workings of the Fellowship, The Gander-*

Flight of the Thirteen Doges of Comus (Louisville, 1886). All quotations taken from p. 74.

13. Moore, *History* 1:276–77.

14. *Daily Mail,* April 28, 1858, p. 1, col. 1.

15. Ibid., April 28, 29, 1858.

16. Ibid., August 31, 1857, p. 1, col. 1.

17. Hoole, *Alias,* p. 114.

18. Thomas S. Woodward, *Woodward's Reminiscences of the Creek, or Muscogee Indians* (Montgomery: Barrett & Wimbish, 1859).

19. *Daily Mail,* April 2, 1858, p. 1, col. 1.

20. Ibid., April 7, 1858, p. 2, col. 1; and April 5, 1858, p. 1, col. 1–2.

21. Ibid., July 17, 1858, p. 1, col. 1.

22. Ibid., July 24, 27, in Hoole, *Alias,* p. 100.

23. Ibid., 29 (February 26, 1859):25.

24. *Daily Mail,* March 14, 1859, p. 1, col. 2; March 16, 1859, p. 1, col. 3. See also Hoole, *Alias,* pp. 120, 229, n. 34.

25. Ibid., March 16, 1859, p. 1, col. 3, 4.

26. Ibid., February 2, 1860, in Kelley, "Life and Writings," p. 163.

27. Lewy Dorman, *Party Politics in Alabama from 1850 through 1860,* Alabama State Department of Archives and History, Historical and Patriotic Series, no. 13 (Wetumpka, Ala., 1935), pp. 143, 145.

28. Ibid., pp. 149, 151.

29. *Spirit* 29 (October 15, 1859):421.

30. H. Montgomery Hyde, *A History of Pornography* (New York: Farrar, Straus & Giroux, 1965), p. 132.

31. *Daily Mail,* January 16, 1860, p. 2, col. 3, in Kelley, "Life and Writings," p. 136.

32. *Daily Mail,* November 24, 1859, p. 2, col. 3.

33. Ibid., December 22, 1859, p. 2, col. 2.

34. Ibid., March 19, 1860, p. 3, col. 1.

35. *Spirit* 30 (April 21, 1860):124.

36. *Daily Mail,* February 18, 1860, p. 2, col. 2.

37. *Montgomery Weekly Mail,* April 20, 1860, in Hoole, *Alias,* pp. 129–30.

38. *Daily Mail,* May 1, 1860, p. 2, col. 2.

39. *Weekly Mail,* February 1, 1860, in Hoole, *Alias,* p. 132.

40. Blum et al., *National Experience,* pp. 332–33.

41. Hoole, *Alias,* p. 134.

42. Ibid., p. 137.

43. Ibid.

44. *Weekly Mail,* September 7, 1860, in Hoole, *Alias,* p. 235,

n. 26. In the *Weekly Mail* for November 9, 1860, p. 1, col. 1, Hooper expressed distress in "Our Unqualified Disapproval and Condemnation" at reports that some citizens of Montgomery had been so rude as to throw eggs at Stephen A. Douglas.

45. In Kelley, "Life and Writings," p. 139.
46. *Daily Mail,* September 10, 1860, in Hoole, *Alias,* pp. 139; 236–37, n. 34, 35.
47. Ibid., November 6, 1860, p. 2, col. 2.
48. Hoole, *Alias,* pp. 140–43.
49. *Weekly Mail,* January 18, 1861, p. 1, col. 1.
50. Hoole, *Alias,* p. 145.
51. Moore, *History,* 1:512.
52. *Daily Mail,* January 18 (dated 12), 1861, in Hoole, *Alias,* p. 147.

Chapter Seven

1. Moore, *History,* 1:525, 527.
2. *Weekly Mail,* January 25 (dated 19), 1861, p. 4, col. 2.
3. Ibid., January 25 (dated 24), 1861, p. 5, col. 1.
4. Moore, *History,* 1:519.
5. *Weekly Mail,* February 8, 1861, in Hoole, *Alias,* pp. 153; 239, n. 12.
6. Kelley, "Life and Writings," p. 76.
7. *Spirit of the Times* 31 (March 2, 1861):52.
8. Hoole, *Alias,* p. 153.
9. Ibid., pp. 157; 248, n. 28.
10. Ibid., pp. 157; 240, n. 23.
11. Kelley, "Life and Writings," p. 179.
12. Hoole, *Alias,* p. 158, n. 31.
13. Kelley, "Life and Writings," pp. 182–83.
14. Hoole, *Alias,* p. 160.
15. In Kelley, "Life and Writings," pp. 330–31. Colonel M. F. Maury had been an associate of the senior Hooper in the Alleghany copper mining venture.
16. Blum et al., *National Experience,* p. 350.
17. Hoole, *Alias,* p. 165.
18. Ibid., pp. 167; 244–45, n. 23.
19. Blum et al., *National Experience,* p. 345.
20. Hoole, *Alias,* p. 171.
21. Ibid., pp. 156, 172.
22. *Gadsden Leader,* February 7, 1891, in Hoole, *Alias,* p. 172.
23. In Hoole, *Alias,* p. 172.
24. Kelley, "Life and Writings," p. 245.

25. Hoole, *Alias,* p. 247, n. 53.

26. Kelley, "Life and Writings," p. 244.

27. Hoole, *Alias,* p. 173.

Chapter Eight

1. *Magnum Opus,* p. 74.

2. Garrett, *Reminiscences,* pp. 527–28.

3. Dorman, *Party Politics,* p. 36, n. 17.

4. Moore, *History,* 1:506–7. Moore describes himself as "a Democrat, a Baptist," 3:776.

5. Annie Mae Hollingsworth, "Johnson J. Hooper, Alabama's Mark Twain, Champion of the Creeks," *Montgomery Advertiser,* March 23, 1931, p. 3.

6. Kelley, "Life and Writings," pp. 200–203.

7. *Daily Mail,* November 21, 1854, p. 2, col. 1.

8. Ibid., May 6, 1858, p. 2, col. 1.

9. *Spirit* 28 (November 13, 1858):475.

10. Whitaker, "The Hooper Family," p. 55. This quotation is taken from Archibald Maclaine Hooper's "William Hooper, Signer of the Declaration of Independence." Hooper's syntax is less clear than that of his son Johnson, and these words may have been uttered by William Hooper's friend Samuel Johnston.

11. *Daily Mail,* April 14, 1859, p. 1, col. 2.

12. Hoole, *Alias,* pp. 181; 249, n. 26.

13. See ibid., pp. 173–76, for a more complete catalog of Hooper reprints and critical references.

14. Joel Campbell Dubose, *Alabama History* (Atlanta: B. F. Johnson, 1908), p. 317.

15. Rhoda Coleman Ellison, *Early Alabama Publications* (University: University of Alabama Press, 1947), p. 74.

16. Eugene Current-Garcia, "Alabama Writers in the Spirit," *Alabama Review* 10 (October 1957):245.

17. Williams, *Literary History of Alabama,* pp. 100–101, 109. See also Peter A. Brannon, "Jons Hooper's Influence in Early State Literature," *Montgomery Advertiser,* Centennial ed., March 15, 1928 (no page number).

18. Christian Messenger, "Southwestern Humorists and Ring Lardner—Sport in American Literature," *Illinois Quarterly* 39 (Fall 1976):5–21.

19. Cecil D. Eby, "Faulkner and the Southwestern Humorists," *Shenandoah* 11 (Autumn 1959):18. See also Carvel Collins, "Faulkner and Certain Earlier Southern Fiction," *College English* 16 (1954):92–94.

20. M. Thomas Inge, "Literary Humor of the Old Southwest: A Brief Overview," *Louisiana Studies* 7 (Summer 1968):142.

21. Alan Gribben, *Mark Twain's Library,* 2 vols. (Boston: G. K. Hall, 1980), 1:322.

22. Samuel Clemens, ed., *Mark Twain's Library of Humor* (New York: Charles L. Webster, 1888; reprint, New York: Garrett Press, 1969).

23. Kenneth Lynn, *Mark Twain and Southwestern Humor* (Boston: Little, Brown & Co., 1959), p. 140.

24. Bernard De Voto, *Mark Twain's America* (Boston, 1951), pp. 255–56.

25. John Rachal, "Scotty Briggs and the Minister: An Idea from Hooper's Simon Suggs?" *Mark Twain Journal* 17 (Summer 1974):10–11.

26. Chittick, *Ring-Tailed Roarers,* p. 167.

27. Blair, *Native,* pp. 102–24.

Selected Bibliography

PRIMARY SOURCES

1. Books

Adventures of Captain Simon Suggs, Late of the Tallapoosa Volunteers. Edited with an introduction by Manly Wade Wellman. Chapel Hill: University of North Carolina Press, 1969.

Dog and Gun; A Few Loose Chapters on Shooting, Among Which Will Be Found Some Anecdotes and Incidents. In *Moore's Rural Handbooks.* New York: A. O. Moore, Agricultural Book Publisher (late C. M. Saxton & Co.), 1858.

Magnum Opus. The Great Book of the University of Comus. The Pandect of our National Hilaritas, Comprising Essays upon the Thirteen Divisions of the Rituals; Sketches of the Tredecim Doges, Authors of the Plan, and a Monitorial Guide to the Workings of the Fellowship, The Gander-Flight of the Thirteen Doges of Comus. Louisville, Ky.: Published under Direction of the Thirteen Doges, 1886.

Read and Circulate: Proceedings of the Democratic and Anti-Know-Nothing Party in Caucus; or the Guillotine at Work, at the Capital, during the Session of 1855–'56. Montgomery, Ala.: Barrett & Wimbish, 1855.

Some Adventures of Captain Simon Suggs, Late of the Tallapoosa Volunteers; Together with "Taking the Census," and Other Alabama Sketches. By a Country Editor. Philadelphia: Carey & Hart, 1846.

The Widow Rugby's Husband, A Night at the Ugly Man's, and Other Tales of Alabama. Philadelphia: A. Hart, 1851.

2. Miscellaneous Pieces

"Colonel Hawkins and the Court." *Ring-Tailed Roarers; Tall Tales of the American Frontier, 1830–1860.* Edited by V. L. O. Chittick. Caldwell, Idaho: The Caxton Printers, 1941.

"Daddy Biggs' Scrape at Cockerell Bend." *Humor of the Old Southwest.* 2d ed. Edited by Hennig Cohen and William B. Dillingham. Athens: University of Georgia Press, 1975.

"In Favor of the Hog." *Yankee Notions* 6 (September 1857).

"A Georgia Major." *Harper's New Monthly Magazine,* December 1854.

"A Night at the Ugly Man's." *Humor of the Old Deep South.* Edited by Arthur Palmer Hudson. New York: Macmillan, 1936.
"Sloshin' About." *Harper's New Monthly Magazine,* October 1854.

SECONDARY SOURCES

1. Books and Parts of Books
Blair, Walter. *Native American Humor.* San Francisco: Chandler, 1960.
De Voto, Bernard. *Mark Twain's America.* Boston: Houghton Mifflin, 1932, 1951. Most authoritative argument for Hooper's influence on Clemens.
Dorman, Lewy. *Party Politics in Alabama from 1850 through 1860.* Alabama State Department of Archives and History. Historical and Patriotic Series, no. 13. Wetumpka, Ala.: Wetumpka Printing Co., 1935. Detailed background of Alabama partisan politics.
Garrett, William. *Reminiscences of Public Men in Alabama.* Atlanta: Plantation Publishing Co., 1872. Source of much of the adverse personal criticism of Hooper.
Hoole, W. Stanley. *Alias Simon Suggs; The Life and Times of Johnson Jones Hooper.* University: University of Alabama Press, 1952. The definitive biography.
Inge, M. Thomas, ed. *The Frontier Humorists; Critical Views.* Hamden, Conn.: The Shoe String Press, 1975. Fine collection of essays on southwestern humor in general, including some that deal with Hooper.
Meine, Franklin J., ed. *Tall Tales of the Southwest; an Anthology of Southern and Southwestern Humor, 1830–1860.* New York: Alfred A. Knopf, 1930. Excellent introduction and anthology.
Moore, Albert Burton. *History of Alabama and Her People.* 3 vols. New York: American Historical Society, 1927. General background with some mention of Hooper as a writer.
Williams, Benjamin Buford. *A Literary History of Alabama; the Nineteenth Century.* Cranbury, N.J.: Associated University Presses, 1979. A dozen pages on Hooper.
Yates, Norris W. *William T. Porter and the Spirit of The Times; A Study of the Big Bear School of Humor.* Baton Rouge: Louisiana State University Press, 1957. Tells as much as is known about Hooper and Porter.

2. Articles
Collins, Carvel. "Faulkner and Certain Earlier Southern Fiction." *College English* 16 (1954):92–97. Minimizes the direct effect of southwestern humor on Faulkner.

Eby, Cecil D. "Faulkner and the Southwestern Humorists." *Shenandoah* 11 (Autumn 1959):13–21. Faulkner shares concerns with the southwestern humorists but transcends them.

Hollingsworth, Annie Mae. "Johnson Jones Hooper, Alabama's Mark Twain, Champion of the Creeks." *Montgomery Advertiser,* March 23, 1931, p. 3.

Hopkins, Robert. "Simon Suggs: A Burlesque Campaign Biography." *American Quarterly* 15 (Fall 1963):459–63. Supplies valuable historical perspective.

Messenger, Christian. "Southwestern Humorists and Ring Lardner— Sport in American Literature." *Illinois Quarterly* 39 (Fall 1976):5–21. Cites parallels in vernacular characterization.

Rachal, John. "Scotty Briggs and the Minister: An Idea from Hooper's Simon Suggs?" *Mark Twain Journal* 17 (Summer 1974):10–11. Detailed analysis of the two writers' use of gambling metaphors.

Whitaker, Fanny Hooper. "The Hooper Family." *North Carolina Booklet* 5 (July 1905):39–71. Reprints Archibald Maclaine Hooper's essay on William Hooper, "The Signer."

3. Thesis

Kelley, Marion. "The Life and Writings of Johnson Jones Hooper." Master's thesis, Alabama Polytechnic Institute, 1934. Excellent source of biographical information and reprinted editorials and letters. Drawn on by Hoole.

Index

Holifield, Joseph A., 82
Hoole, W. Stanley, 4, 87, 91, 93,
  131, 140
Hooper, Adolphus Stanford
  (son), 87, 112, 131, 133, 135
Hooper, Archibald Maclaine (father), 2–3, 69, 80, 143
Hooper, Charlotte DeBerniere
  (mother), 1, 69
Hooper, George (brother), 2–3,
  4, 6, 7–8, 80
Hooper, George (grandfather),
  1–2
Hooper, John (brother), 2
Hooper, Johnson Jones, life and
  career: advocates secession,
  124, 125; Alleghany Mining
  Company venture, 115–16,
  143; attends Southern Commercial Convention, 102–105;
  "beau ideal" of southern newspaper editors, 87, 138; birth,
  2; challenges rival editor to
  duel, 109, 142; "Champion of
  the Creeks," 5–6, 138, 141;
  death, 135–37; defeated for reelection to solicitorship of
  Ninth district, 79–80; edits Lafayette's *East Alabamian,* 8, 9;
  elected secretary for Provisional Confederate Congress,
  128–29, 138; elected solicitor
  of Ninth District, 69–70, 138;
  first known publication, "Anthony Milan's Launch," 2–3;
  Hooper's *Montgomery Mail*
  backs American party candidates, 90–92; joins law firm of
  brother George in Lafayette, 7–
  8; joins Roman Catholic
  Church, 133–34; leaves *Alabama Journal* to edit *Chambers
  County Tribune,* 49–50; literary
  influence, 144–46; literary rep-

utation, 143–44; loses election
  to secretaryship of newly reor-
  ganized Confederate Senate,
  134–35; marriage, 8; moves to
  Montgomery, works on *Alabama Journal,* 48; moves to
  Richmond with Confederate
  government, 130–31; obituaries, 136–37; physical description, 75–76; plagued by ill-
  health and financial difficulty
  with *Mail,* 92–94; resigns editorship of *East Alabamian,*
  moves to Wetumpka to edit the
  Whig, 48; returns to Montgomery to edit the *Mail,* 81; sells
  interest in *Mail,* 130; "Senior
  Editor" of *Mail,* 95–96; Suggs
  stories first appear in *Spirit of
  the Times,* 28–29; takes census
  of Tallapoosa County, 7

WORKS—POETRY:
"Anthony Milan's Launch," 2–
  3, 8

WORKS—PROSE:
"Alabama Lawyer, An," 50–51
"Alligator Story, An," 73–74
"Big Brothel—A Peep into the
  Bowers of Free Love, A"
  (editorial), 117–18
"Captain Attends a Camp Meet-
  ing, The," 36–38, 44, 139,
  145–46
"Captain Is Arraigned Before
  'A Jury of His Country,'
  The," 38–39
"Captain McSpadden: The Irish
  Gentleman in Purschute of
  a Schule, Etc.," 52

PS
1999
H25
Z87

Somers, Paul
Johnson

DATE DUE—